The Newsroom
Confessions

Bob LeMoullec

PAGE PUBLISHING, INC.
New York, NY

First originally published by Page Publishing, Inc. 2014

ISBN 978-1-62838-632-5 (pbk)
ISBN 978-1-62838-633-2 (digital)

Printed in the United States of America

Contents

One

No One Ever Said to Me You Ought to Be in Radio

It's funny, but it never dawned on me that I'd have a career in radio and television news. I listened to radio throughout my childhood. I also looked at the stars, but I never thought of going to any of them.

I traveled in a career fog through my early years. Sometime after college, I thought I'd like to be a newspaper reporter or columnist. I was inspired by some of the pre-Murdoch *New York Post* writers, including James Wechsler and Max Lerner along with syndicated columnist Mary McGrory. I had a long way to go if I wanted to get there.

My journey into the news business began when I heard an ad on the radio pushing a broadcasting school. I checked with the Veterans Administration. It turned out the four years I spent at college didn't eat up all my GI Bill benefits, meaning I could take this course for free. I didn't want to pay for it myself, especially not knowing the outcome in advance. The idea of a career in radio seemed a bit far-fetched.

The school's director said I had to audition for the class. As it turned out, they put a mirror under your nose, and if they found steam, you passed. Maybe not literally, but you catch my drift. I couldn't have sounded shittier. Who knew? I never heard myself on tape.

I was sort of a too-fast talking Leo Gorcey. You may remember the guy with the turned up hat from the Dead End Kids. That's him. He had a nasal voice and a thick New York accent.

There were guys there with lisps, speech defects, stutters—you name it. One guy had Tourette's. "Uck, fuck, uck . . . fuck, suck . . . uck."

Somehow it miraculously disappeared when the "on air" light went on. Then the light went off, "Poon, cho-cha, suck, toooowhat." I thought he was kidding, but he moved his head like Ray Charles when he went off. That had to be legitimate.

Another media wannabe shaved his arms and put make-up on, ostensibly to prepare himself for a television career. One sounded great, but he literally couldn't read. He figured he'd just play records and never get asked to read a commercial. I'm sure they filled out the application for him while he was opening his wallet.

I figured even if I never got a job in the business, I'll sound better when I'm done. What did I have to lose? The Federal Communications Commission required anyone on the air to get a third-class broadcasting license. A copy of everyone's license was posted next to the transmitter where an inspector could see it. No license equaled no work. The school prepared you for the third-class test. It wasn't easy. Some prospective "talents" never passed. Luckily, I made it on the first try.

The school also turned me on to some low-paying, very part-time work. Let's see. I covered a demonstration in Philadelphia where I barely broke even by paying my way down there. That was for WBAB in Babylon, Long Island. I made a few bucks covering election nights. I did some disc-jockeying in connection with the school. I also spun gospel records at WGNY. Not bad for an unprincipled agnostic.

I also did some booth announcing for a local cable company. That's where you announce at the beginning and end of a program, "This game is brought to you by," followed by a list of sponsors that probably hoped for a more professional voice for their money.

WBAB was a rock station that simulcast on AM and FM until they switched the AM into WGNY. News was only an FCC requirement to them. Someone in the newsroom would tape newscasts from WHLI and rewrite them. It was completely unethical. WBAB had no wire service. It relied on light news services such as the *Source* or *Zodiac*. That's really light.

Some of their newscasts actually led with UFO sightings and otherworldly incidents that were treated as hard, cold facts. At the time, the real Amityville horror case was going on. Amityville was just down the road; a godsend for these guys. The FCC required all broadcasters to do news and public affairs. It didn't care about content. There was a very good talk show with good guests that Joel Martin did. Perhaps the most newsworthy was having the Billy Hayes family coming in a number of times. Their son was in a Turkish prison for trying to smuggle hashish out of that country. The idea was to keep his story alive. The parents used the station to pressure the United States government to do something. Billy Hayes eventually escaped and wrote a book about it called *Midnight Express*.

When I wasn't working outside of my day job, which was practically always, I would do voice exercises and practice reading out loud. I was never satisfied with the way I sounded, but I did improve. At one point, I sent out an audition tape that I thought was pretty clever. This was 1974. I chose the top ten songs of a given week. Mine was December 31, 1960. I thought a show like that would hide the flaws in my delivery.

I got no takers. Six years later, I heard some DJ doing *my* show. I guess I would have been angrier at being ripped off, except I ripped off Norm N' Night's book for the information I used on my tape.

Two

Minimum Wage Rock and Roll

The WRKL main office had a seedy look to it. I'm sure the carpet had cat piss on it. The room had that smell. I know cats go in litter boxes. Not here. This feline named Vin had the run of the place in exchange for keeping the mice out. No one fed it. No one changed the box. It was Vin that met me at the front door.

It was early October 1978. I noticed a woman working in the corner was all made up with her hair professionally done. Everyone else had a one bounced check away from being homeless look. I found out later, Barrie Lipscomb was canoodling around on her husband with the boss and any other interested takers.

Some of the "talent" wore rumpled flannel shirts. Others had short-sleeve shirts that were also rumpled. Most wore jeans that could bear some washing. I wore a jacket and tie.

No shirt. Just kidding, but I would have felt more at home that way.

There was something else I noticed. Dozens of awards and plaques were hanging on the walls. There was a DuPont Columbia award for the best political coverage in the nation; an Edward R. Morrow award from the Radio and Television News Directors Association; along with numerous other honors from the New York State Broadcasters Association and the Associated Press. The plaques also served as a border for a huge plate glass window that looked into the air studio. Inside was a disc jockey doing his show. He had a very good, deep, rich sound. I listened to WRKL for the first time after I scheduled my interview.

The DJs sounded very professional. They were all much better than I was. There were no "pukers," which is how some Top Forty jocks sound. To give you an idea of what I mean, Cousin Brucie is a classic puker. The news people, with a couple of exceptions, didn't sound that great. They were all better than I was though.

The main office looked kind of beat up. There were several old metal desks spaced around the room, which measured something like twenty by forty feet. Each had an electric typewriter. There was a row of executive offices on one side. The narrow newsroom took up the entire other side of the building. A small production room abutted the air studio and the on air news booth.

The building was constructed out of concrete blocks. Inside, they were piled on top of one another instead of the usual pattern where each vertical joint is centered over the block above and below it. The result were cracks in the walls too numerous to count.

"I'm here to see Bob Marvin," I cheerfully told the receptionist whose desk was oddly placed in the middle of the room. "A Mrs. Heitman from unemployment set it up so he'll give me an overview of the business." How I got to the unemployment office doesn't matter at this point.

Mrs. Heitman was a counselor in the Spring Valley branch. I told her I planned to change careers. I wanted nothing to do with the insurance business where I squandered seven years as a commercial lines underwriter.

I never imagined I'd spend a big chunk of my life wearing a jacket and tie, pushing paper in dreary offices, but that's what it was. It was time I did something else. I could always go back to the drudgery if I failed.

I was always fascinated with radio. My mother knew everything about every kind of music. She would have it playing all day. She bought classical records from the supermarket. Back in the day, they came in sets with a new one coming out every week. That's one way we were exposed to composers such as Beethoven, Saint Saens, Dvorak, and so forth. She also had recordings of Thelonius Monk, Charlie Parker, Dizzy Gillespie, Peggy Lee, and the like.

I saw Louis Armstrong in concert before I saw anyone else. It was a great musical education. I loved music. If I had talent, I might have been a musician or a songwriter. I guess that's like saying if that horse wasn't a gelding, he'd be a stud. Even geldings have fantasies.

Early radio also had some dramas and comedies that eventually made it to television. When I was four or five, I would press my face against the speaker to try to see the little people inside talking. My mother insisted there were no little people. It's the first time I can remember not believing her.

So I kept looking without any luck.

On her own, Mrs. Heitman, saint that she was, set me up with an appointment with WRKL radio's general manager. Bob Marvin would talk to me about radio in general and what opportunities, if any, were out there. As chance would have it, a part-time disc jockey/producer had just told Mr. Marvin to go fuck himself as he walked out for a better job in Poughkeepsie—of all places.

We passed each other at the door.

Bob Marvin was a fairly well-built bald man with his hair closely cropped on the side. He had the bearing of someone who had worked out at one time. Turns out he was in the Marine Corps. There was a sign on his wall that read "God made only a few good heads . . . the rest he covered with hair." He also had a cat of nine tails mounted next to a bull whip.

We connected as veterans. When he spoke, he treated every word like each was something special; not to be confused with the previous or next one. He would, on occasion, leave a half second between words. I guess you might call it over articulating. His droning voice was a bit whiney.

I mentioned the disc jockey we could hear through his speakers had a great sound.

"Yes, he has everything you need to make it in broadcasting: a low voice and no brains." He also gave me an impromptu critique of his sales force. "They're a bunch of drooling imbeciles. They can't sell pussy in a whorehouse. My secretary, Barrie Lipscomb, will have her duties expanded. I expect her to straighten this place out."

We chatted for about a half hour before I was unexpectedly offered a job.

"You'll be a part-time disc jockey, production engineer, and anything else that needs to be done around the radio station. There's little money in the budget, but there'll be plenty of hours, so you won't starve."

I was in luck. Bob Marvin didn't ask for an air check or audition tape. He just had a bit of advice. "You'll be on the air Saturday afternoon. Jeff Baker is our morning man and chief station engineer. He'll make sure you can run the board. He'll also show you how to put the commercials together when you're doing production work. One more thing, keep it low and keep it slow."

My DJ fantasy quickly turned into a harsh wake-up call. I thought I'd be lying around, picking out my favorite records, putting out a show my large listening audience would really enjoy. Most people think that's all there is to it. That's the way it was in the big time: You chose a song. You handed the disk to an engineer, said a few words, and relaxed. No, Bob. This was 1978. This was small market radio. You were the engineer.

Here's how it went: You sat at a board. The one at WRKL had ten "pots" or dials. Two pots went to the two turntables on either side of your chair. A third was for your mike. There were two more pots for two tape recorders. There were a sixth and seventh for two cart machines. Carts loosely resemble super eight cassettes. An eighth was for the "hotline" table where a mid-day talk show was done in the same studio. There was another to bring up the news booth. The last brought up the production studio. That was complicated enough.

Now you had to remember to have the mike pot up

when you flipped on your microphone. If you didn't, your "on air" light would be on, but you'd be transmitting dead air.

There were two meters on the board that let you know how hot your decibel levels were. You'd try to keep needle bouncing from the left, which was minus, against the "red," which was peak. That would be to eliminate distortion. The needle on Phil Spector records stayed at the peak all the way through without budging to either side. That's what people meant when they said his productions were "walls of sound." Even if your levels were registering, that didn't mean you were going out over the air.

Are you confused yet?

You had to remember to turn the pots all the way down to "cue" when you were cuing a record. Otherwise, the audience would hear the *wah wah* of the beginning of a record as you got to the right spot. You needed about five seconds of leeway. If you cued it too close to the beginning, the record will groan until it gets up to speed. If you were too far from the start, you'd get dead air. You also couldn't forget that if it's an LP, you needed your turntable to be set to 33 1/3 RPM. If it's a single, make sure it was on 45 RPM. WRKL also had some old 78 RPM records on the playlist, so beware.

So you're playing a record. You better have another ready to go on the other turntable. That seemed easy enough, except you had to deal with a logbook with a list of commercials that had to either be read live on the air or played on the cart machine.

While your record was playing, you'd be going through the traffic or commercial book. The ads had to be done at the time they were logged. You were also reading "lost pets," which had a sounder before the introduction. Then there was the WRKL Community Events Calendar, the time, and the temperature.

If you had the early shift, you'd be going through a folder looking for school lunches of the day. At least there were no obits. There was nothing worse than a gloomy undertaker pretending to be real depressed as he wrapped up someone's life in thirty cheerless seconds. Some small market radio stations did these.

You should be updating the weather, especially in the morning or in the case of an upcoming unusual event. You shouldn't open your mike between records without mentioning the call letters. There was also a newscast you threw to every half hour. Some of the casts were sponsored, so you had to have a billboard ready to read. Most of the records we played were less than two minutes long, so you didn't have much time.

I eventually learned to avoid dead air. I also learned to talk under the musical intros of some records. They would all have the length of the record posted on the label. There would also be the intro time. If it said thirteen seconds, you had the time to mention the weather underneath or do the call letters or just talk up the artist. We'd use the instrumentals to back time into the newscasts. There was plenty of time to talk over them.

Sometimes the engineers, Jeff Baker or Neil Mazur, would come in and work on the board in the middle of my show. While it was a royal pain in the ass, the radio station had a great sound. It was nothing like the muffled sound you get from some AM stations.

Then you also had the tours. Groups including cub

scouts, brownies, and grade school classes came to the studio to learn about radio. They watched you through the glass like you were a zoo animal. Sometimes they were allowed into the studio to chat in between records so their parents and teachers could get the thrill of hearing their charges on the air. The big coup was giving each kid a 45 RPM record that no self-respecting radio station would ever play in a million years. You'd be shocked at how much music shit record companies put out that you'll never hear. The Norman Beatoff Choir sang other people's hits. How about "Can't Smile Without You" by Gino Cunico? Maybe the Charisma Band doing "Boogie People"? Here's one: "In Heaven There Is No Beer" by the group Clean Living. Vanguard records put that one out. Wasn't Joan Baez on Vanguard? Columbia Records put out the Charisma Band record. I don't remember Gino's label. I'm sure these people were elated to be signed. Never heard of them? You're not alone. I'd pick up these records in the parking lot after the youngsters finished using them as Frisbees. That shows they had taste. We'd hand the same records out to the next group.

There was a format you had to stick to. WRKL played mostly million sellers. We were supposed to come out with a happy song after the news. Bob Marvin said since the newscasts tended to be mostly unhappy, it was important that the music picked up the spirits of the listener. A "clock" or wheel was posted next to the console. It reminded you that 25 percent of the songs we played had to be "current." In WRKL's case, "current" meant the most recently added. By definition, new songs hadn't sold a million copies yet, so we'd wait several months before they were on our playlist.

Looking at the top five songs in early October 1978

when I started: "Boogie, Oogie, Oogie" was number one; followed by the Little River Band's "Reminiscing"; the Commodores, "Three Times a Lady"; "Summer Nights" by John Travolta and Olivia Newton-John; and "You Needed Me" by Anne Murray. "Boogie, Oogie, Oogie" will never see the light of day at WRKL. The other four may not be on our playlist until around Christmas.

Another 25 percent of the selections were MOR or Middle of the Road songs from the seventies. Most disco was out. The other 25 percent were from the sixties, 20 percent were fifties hits, and the final 5 percent were pre-fifties.

The decades had to be mixed. Two selections from the same decade should never be played in succession. A male vocal couldn't follow a male vocal. Groups shouldn't follow groups. We played vocal hits only. Instrumentals were only used to lead into newscasts. We mixed tempos for variety.

As Bob Marvin would say, "Smile when you talk on the air. If you don't have something good to say, don't say it and don't talk too much. The biggest sign of an amateur is the person who thinks he has to keep talking."

There were some million sellers we weren't allowed to play, like Paul Anka's "Having My Baby," which Bob Marvin somehow found offensive. I found that odd since we had Squeeze's "I'm Touching Myself and Thinking of You" and the similarly themed "Turning Japanese" by the Vapors on the playlist.

I got some advice from the other DJs. If you have to take a leak, play Harry Chapin's "Taxi." That's around seven minutes long. If you really, really have to make number two, play Frankie Valle's "Swearin' to God." For some reason, we had the disco version which was about eleven minutes long—

19

that was reserved for people who had just eaten Thai food or were fruitarians.

I was told by Jeff Baker, "Don't play them too often. There are other DJs here."

Don MacLean's "American Pie" was also on the playlist. That was over eight and a half minutes long. "MacArthur Park" by Richard Harris and the Eagles' "Lyin' Eyes" were two more favorites of those who really had to go. How about Iron Butterfly's "In-a-gadda-da-vida," which took up a whole album side? Way too heavy for this place.

"Hey Jude" was not on the playlist. Bob Marvin thought the long ending was too annoying.

One of the daredevils who changed the lights on the thousand-foot towers behind the radio station came into the studio when I was on the air to tell me he was done. I had to take a leak, so I asked him to segue to the next record for me while I was in the men's room. I had the record cued. I told him to turn the pot down on the record that was ending and just hit the button on the other turntable.

I couldn't believe the look of panic in his face. In a million years, I would never climb those towers. He did it without breaking a sweat, yet he couldn't put a record on the air. I told him it was okay, and I held it in until my shift was over.

I'll be honest. There was no way I'd take a newspaper to the men's room with a long record on the turntable. With my luck, it would start skipping when I'm, shall we say dropping deuce, and I'd be two-stepping into the studio with a trail of toilet paper behind me.

I was in heaven playing these records. Eventually, they started getting stale. I always looked forward to new gold records to be added to the playlist. All the DJs felt the same. Until something new came along, our motto became, "All shit, all the time."

This was an awful lot for me to absorb. My parents didn't even let us touch the TV set when we were kids. I was six years old when we became among the first on our block in Brooklyn to have one. So there was a certain mystique to it. Couple this with the natural panic you felt early in your career when the "on the air" light went on, and you had a recipe for disaster.

There was the inevitable dead air between records and my reading whatever came up on the logbook. There was the occasional studio noise when I accidently left my mike on. I started records at the wrong speed more often than I care to remember. I played commercials out of order because I didn't have a record cued, meaning I had to go with a prerecorded ad rather than read something live. You can't cue a record and read at the same time. At least I couldn't.

I stumbled through the lost pets and calendars because the secretary's handwriting was illegible. I couldn't understand how the other DJs could get through these without missing a beat. At least the school lunches we had to read were printed in advance. Some of the newscasts were so long that it necessitated a large stack of carts with sound bites of whoever to be placed in front of us. I had to listen to the news to make sure when the anchor pointed to me, I hit the right one. The carts were numbered and I had the script, but that didn't matter.

Paying attention left me with hardly any time to find a "happy" record. I also wanted to play something I felt the listener would like. Anthology albums were a good bet. If

I grabbed "American Graffiti" off the shelf, I'd have about forty choices but little time to choose.

"Let's see. I haven't played 'The Stroll' in a while. No, too slow. Play 'Crying in the Chapel' out of a newscast? No way. I hate Bobby Freeman's 'Do You Want to Dance.' I stole that record from Woolworths when I was in the seventh grade and played it to death. Now I cringe whenever I hear it. How's that for punishment. 'Get a Job'? No. I don't want to give Bob Marvin any ideas. Okay, 'Maybe Baby.' That's it."

My downfall was I thought too much. Everybody needed a place to suck at the beginning of their career. This was it for me.

Even with the wheel, the playlist could get out of control. Our morning DJ loved country music. That meant plenty of Johnny Cash, Freddie Fender, and Dolly Parton hits. Our evening jock was black. He opted for Motown and Stax. Our afternoon DJ, Steve Possell, called it "shit-kicking in the morning, ass-kicking at night."

So what was the worst episode I ever had? How about being in such a rush that I accidently played the flip side of Kyu Sakamoto's "Sukiyaki." "Sukiyaki" was a million seller in the early sixties. While it had a Western melody, the "B" side made Yoko Ono sound like Johnny Mathis. This was absolutely the worst song on the planet.

Besides the usual panic you'd feel if this was happening to you, I didn't have another record cued. I couldn't get out of it, and I couldn't let this horror show play to the end. I began looking for another record—fast.

"Let's see. Well, I won't play 'Get a Job.'"

Meanwhile, a red-faced Bob Marvin with veins bulging in his neck charged into the studio screaming, "What the fuck is that? Get that shit off! Goddammit! Fuck! Get it off."

Wait. Did I forget to turn my mike off? No, I didn't. *Whew*!

This was only one incident that put me on the fast track to the news department.

Three

How to Do Award-Winning News on the Cheap

December 28, 1980

Most of the newsrooms in the country were probably leading with President Carter breaking his collar bone in a skiing accident at Camp David. I didn't know there were ski slopes at Camp David. I didn't even know President Carter skied. I imagined what happened:

Carter was on skis, moving quickly, surrounded by trees and secret servicemen. He was thinking about his crushing loss last month to Ronald Reagan. "How could I lose to this actor? How could I?" There was a rock obstruction in the president's path. "Was it the hostages . . . the economy . . . it was bad when I got here. Remember Gerald Ford's Whip Inflation Now buttons? How could I lose?" He hit the rock.

Ooops . . . Owwwww! I would write the words *shit* and *fuck* here, but I didn't think the president ever cursed.

In the meantime, I was on the news desk trying to find enough local stories to get us through three half-hour-plus news blocks in the morning. If I couldn't "localize" the Carter story, it would have to be moved down in the newscast.

The rationale was if our audience wanted world and national stories, there were plenty of other radio stations where they could find them. Our slogan was "Rockland news comes first."

I managed to get the Carter story at the top of the newscast by tracking down a local doctor who never met the president but who had fixed enough broken collar bones to tell me what went into fixing the president's. I got three tape cuts and wrote three versions of the story. Maybe I could find someone nearby who broke his or her collarbone skiing, and they could describe their experience and, hopefully, the pain. That would be a *with* story good for three sound bites. Maybe someone around here had skied on the hills around Camp David. I know. It's a stretch.

There was no end to what you can do to localize world and national news. Of course, there were the staples that would beef up the newscasts. They included ethnic issues. We had the largest Hasidic community outside of Williamsburg in the world. We also had one of the largest Haitian populations. We had Catholics. That made the pope a local story. Then there were taxes along with labor problems, business happenings, and the like. We had two nuclear power plants just across the Hudson River. Three Mile Island was fresh in people's minds, so many are afraid of nuclear power.

The weather was usually a winner. We were going through

the coldest spell in recent memory. Temperatures had been hovering at around zero for the past few days. That means we'd put out a number of the usual stories about avoiding frostbite, tenants having problems not getting heat, and the high cost of fuel.

You know the five Ws—who, what, where, when, and why—plus the how. The sixth *W* is "why are we doing the story?"

I had a worse problem than just the big freeze out we'd been experiencing. My beat-up bright orange Volkswagen Bug with black bumpers hated cold weather. When I said beat up, this was a real pile of shit. The floor in the back was missing, so passengers had to ride with their feet propped against the back seat. The front floor on the passenger side wasn't too safe either. The front passenger seat was worn down where I propped my elbow up when I drove. There was about one hundred forty thousand miles of bad road on the odometer.

I didn't ask much from my car. I just wanted it to start when I turned it over and I needed a radio. An AM was enough for me. My battery was on life support. I couldn't afford a new one. Forget about paying for an alternator if that was the issue.

Big problems meant big solutions and big bucks. I made small bucks. At that point, the answer to my prayers was a battery charger I picked up at an auto parts store. Every night, I hooked it into a power outlet in the newsroom. I ran the cables through the partially opened window with the other end attached to the battery under the VW's open hood.

Everyone froze their asses off, so I could keep the window open enough that it didn't crush the cable. There were no complaints for good reason. They related. One who was allergic to cats lived in a basement apartment in a home with cats. We had a DJ who literally lived in his car. Life was rough if you wanted to work at a radio station in the boonies.

At least this piece of shit had a chance to start so I could go home to my small apartment once my shift was over. At worst, it would be yet another night on the couch in the main lobby.

Besides the bitter cold, we got a drought warning from the Spring Valley Water Company. In the middle of winter, who cared? I did. It was a story.

I was the night editor. Sometimes I was still a disc jockey. Other times, I hosted a local talk show called the "WRKL Hotline." I also worked as the afternoon news anchor at WRNW-FM across the river in Briarcliff Manor. That was in Westchester County. You had to string together several shitty, low-paying jobs if you wanted to stay in the business but didn't want to fall behind in your rent.

Last year, I worked a few weeks at an insurance office owned by Stan Drescher. He mentioned a few times that his niece, Fran, had bit parts in some movies including *Saturday Night Fever*. I didn't have the heart to tell him I never heard of her. Stan's claim to fame was the hundreds of clocks with "Relieve the Pressure, Insure with Drescher" emblazoned on them that were hanging on walls of businesses around the county.

My social life? Forget it. I juggled three women on the fringes of my life. Believe me when I say it wasn't easy. You know the Johnny Lee song, "Looking for Love in All the Wrong Places"? That was me.

As night editor, I gathered and wrote the morning news.

I also anchored newscasts every half hour during daylight. WRKL was a daytime AM radio station. That meant we went off the air at sunset.

There was a lot to do. Again, there was a shitload of news time to fill in the morning. Try three thirty-five-minute newscasts at six, seven, and eight. In order to make it work, you needed at least twenty stories on the desk with two to three versions each. To make it happen, I'd follow up stories left by the afternoon people. I'd also freshen up some of the stuff we used in the afternoon with updates and rewrites.

I called every police station in the county at some point. Calls were made on every shift. We had a number of separate police departments. Most would tell you what was going on. With others, you had to go there in person and look at the day book. It told you exactly who was arrested or aided and when. Police were required by law to show you the day book. I also worked with reporters and stringers after they returned from meetings and other events that were covered in the evening. I'd either fix or rewrite their copy before they recorded what we call wraps. Generally, a wrap consisted of one or two or three sentences by the reporter, the voice of the interviewee, then one or two sentences by the reporter followed by a lockout that goes, "Joe Reporter, WRKL, news, Wherever."

I'd leave a couple of wraps or voicers for the morning. It could be an update, or it could be a rewrite of a decent story on the wires. We always counted down, three, two, one before going on tape.

From Monday through Thursday, I worked from seven to about two in the morning. I was rarely done at two. Sundays, I came in at around two thirty in the afternoon and worked till around eleven. I could leave early because we had no one out covering meetings.

On Sunday, I was also the afternoon news anchor. The challenge was to fill five minutes of news at the top of the hour and three minutes at the bottom with enough local stories to keep all of us happy. We all set the highest standards for ourselves. I closed with a thirty-minute newscast before going off the air.

The key here, again, was local news. It was a chore if you think about it, especially in a small community like Rockland County. This was made possible because there was a system in place that kept us on top of virtually every story. We also had a self-imposed mandate to stay ahead of the newspaper. We saw the *Journal News* as our main competition in Rockland. WGRC was the other radio station in Rockland. It was a dollar-a-holler operation. They did a good job, and their reporters were every bit as good as ours—but no one listened to them.

We had five separate systems to follow up stories. I'm not sure who put them in place. I'm sure it had been tweaked many times by our current news director, Rich Mendelson. I'll give him the credit.

This was the winning formula that got us the reputation of being the best radio news operation in New York—bar none: Our assignment board was a giant calendar covered with plastic that sat on a wall opposite the long news desk. On Sunday, the *Journal News* published a list of meetings and upcoming events for the week. Newsworthy events were written on the board in grease pencil. Upcoming demonstrations, trials, etc., were also put on the board. Mendelson decided in advance whether it was to be covered by a reporter or over the phone. He usually came in Sunday night and filled it out. This way, our news people would be able to call and get their assignments for the week.

There was the agenda box. Clerks from Rockland's various municipalities mailed us agendas for their upcoming meetings. The interesting ones were put in the box.

We had a date book. This was for events that would happen in more than a week. When it got close, it was posted on the assignment board. Follow-ups were put in a future file. For instance, if a local mayor said he'll start towing illegally parked cars on the first of the month, we'd put the story in the future file and cover the story on that date. The follow sheet was key. This is how we communicated to the next person who took over the desk. Sure, we spoke to each other. However, there was no substitute for leaving information on stories we'd been working on along with which newsmakers were called and who returned the call. You could also leave story ideas and unused tape for the next person.

I'd go through the elements of the five systems I just wrote about for story ideas.

Another "sky is falling" story couldn't hurt. The morning anchor/reporter brought in some tape from a United Water spokeswoman I could use about a drought that was parching the county.

"We're using three million gallons a day more than this time last year." So I went to the Rolodex to round up the usual Kumbaya conservationist for suggestions.

"Less frequent flushing of toilets will save a substantial amount of water. I'd say about seven gallons per flush." My mind went into a tangent.

"Why not tell everyone to go shit in the woods? How about relieving yourself while you're taking a short shower?"

The conservationist suggested, "You could wash dishes in a pan instead of the sink."

I thought, "*How about splashing your clothes in a pan with one of those old washboards?*"

I'll play along and mention a navy shower. When you're at sea, fresh water is very limited. You get wet, shut off the water, and soap down. Then you turn it on again and rinse. That saves three and a half gallons per shower. That's half a flush.

Four

A Most Gruesome
Double Murder

I was in the newsroom for about an hour when the phone rang. "I'm Dave Garey. I used to be a disc jockey at WRKL."

His real name was Dave Zechnowitz. He told me he was between jobs as a talk show host. He'd been at radio stations in more states than I care to count. He was another one of those in the business who lived out of his car most of the time. He sounded like he was in shock.

"I've been listening to your newscasts, and you haven't mentioned this. I guess you don't have the story. Two friends of my parents were murdered last night. They're Arnold and Elaine Sohn. They were at a party with my parents at another friend's house until early this morning. We all live in Spring Valley. It was a fiftieth birthday party for my father. Every

Sunday morning, the Sohns pick up bagels and come over. Today, they didn't show up. The police are at the house now. I hear Arnold was beaten to death, and Elaine was drowned in the bathtub."

I started to roll tape for some sound bites. If I could confirm the story, I'd put it on the air. Garey didn't want to be recorded. *Dammit!*

There was nothing on the scanner. That's understandable since the crime apparently happened overnight, and the cops weren't called until this morning. Police checks were another story.

I made my calls at around three o'clock in the afternoon and was only told about a fatal accident involving a former captain of the Ramapo High School cheerleading squad. Eighteen-year-old Bonnie Harris was an Olympic hopeful in the vault. It was a one-car crash. No seatbelts. Three others in the car were hurt.

"Anything else?"

"No."

Some cops were the fucking worst when it came to giving out information.

They liked to think they had three balls with their "under siege" mentality.

I had a few minutes before I went on the air with the final newscast of the day. As I mentioned, we're a daytimer. In the winter, we went off the air at five.

I called Spring Valley and one of the sergeants picked up. "Yes, there's a homicide investigation going on." I didn't have time to complain that he screwed me when I called just over an hour ago. Not that he gave a shit.

I rolled tape while thinking, *You fucking twat. How about*

sucking my balls.

We never use police on tape unless we're desperate. They're too boring.

"There's one male, one female, possible victims of foul play. The male is fifty years of age. The female is forty-seven years of age. Place of occurrence is 38 Jill Lane, Monsey, New York. Circumstances are still under investigation. The cause is undetermined. That's all I have."

What does "possible victims of foul play" mean, jerkoff? In other words, Mr. Sohn kept bashing his head until he passed out? Mrs. Sohn decided to drown herself at the same time?

The shitty quote was all I had. I needed to put something on the air. Anything. So I used it.

I called Rich Mendelson to let him know what was going on. He would come in later to fill out the assignment board anyway, so he could man the fort. I had all night to put the morning news together. That meant I could go to the scene when we went off the air. I knew it was late. I'd probably only get neighbors who'd tell me how shocked and afraid they were and how nice the Sohns were.

If they weren't still at the Sohns house when I get there, I'd call District Attorney Kenneth Gribetz and Medical Examiner Dr. Frederick Zugibe when I got back to the station. I had their home numbers, and they were great with the news media.

My car started. *Thank you! Thank you!*

The house on 38 Jill Lane was your typical high ranch. The bedrooms sat over a two-car garage. There was probably a den a few steps down when you walked in. The police weren't letting anyone inside. It was dark, but it appeared the house sat on about a half acre of land. The property was protected by yellow crime-scene tape and a couple of officers standing guard.

I was in luck. *Journal News* reporter Mike Barlow was there. Most reporters will share their notes, unless they're working on something exclusive. Mike came through for me.

"I heard it's really gruesome in there. There's blood all over the place."

"Gribetz knew the couple. He said Arnold Sohn was beaten so badly, he couldn't recognize him."

Mike read some Gribetz quotes to me I could use.

"This was an extremely brutal and savage attack. Elaine Sohn was found floating in a bathtub in a nearby bathroom. Both victims were gagged with men's socks and were fully clothed. If this was a burglary, it's one for the books. I've never seen a burglary as brutal as this."

Mike said Dr. Zugibe told him there was so much blood on Arnold Sohn's head that he doesn't know if he was shot as well as beaten.

I saw Spring Valley Police Chief Adam Krainiak. He'd go on tape. He checked his notes. "The couple left a party at around one thirty in the morning. Their bodies were discovered at 11:30 AM. Arnold's blood was on two bedroom drawers. Apparently his head was smashed against them a number of times. The couple's coats were on the bedroom floor.

"That could mean they were met by the intruders almost immediately upon arriving home. The house wasn't ransacked. That could mean the killers weren't there very long. Most burglars, when they're surprised, will flee to avoid a confrontation. They rarely commit murder."

"Were there signs of forcible entry?"

"No. The Sohns may have left the door unlocked when they left."

I left three wraps when I got back to the radio station. I put enough stuff on the desk for the morning. I got home at four o'clock.

December 29, 1980

Most of the heavy lifting on this story was done already by our reporters by the time I got to work.

Arnold Sohn was a furniture salesman at Bloomingdale's in New York City. The couple had two children. Mark Sohn is a student at the State University of New York at Buffalo. He was in Florida for the break. He's twenty. Sheryl Sohn is twenty-three. She lived at home but stayed at a friend's house a block away while her parents were being killed.

I found some people who knew the younger Sohns. I was told Sheryl hung out with a bad element. She was a regular at a sleaze bar called the Camelot in downtown Spring Valley.

One person said it must have been one of her druggie friends who did it. Another told me she had a bad temper: "Like the time she threw her brother out of his bedroom window when they were fighting."

She was a big girl, tipping the scales at about two hundred twenty-five pounds. Mark, on the other hand, was undersized.

I was told she hated her mother but was very close to her father. Someone else told me he made fun of her size, calling her Hoss after the Dan Blocker character, Hoss Cartwright, on the TV show "Bonanza."

Dr. Zugibe completed his autopsy. He was a fifty-ish forensic pathologist who had been published many times. His tenor voice along with his white hair, goatee, and slight lisp when he pronounced his *S*'s gave him the demeanor of a mad scientist. It was common knowledge he kept human fingers in one of his drawers. That didn't hurt the image.

Every conversation with him was a learning experience. He'd point out things you never thought of. I did a story about a possible suicide where the victim supposedly sliced her wrists. He pointed out it couldn't be suicide because "When you slit your own wrists, you go from the thumb to the pinky. In this case, the slice went from the pinky to the thumb. This was no suicide." I always looked forward to speaking with him.

He studied the Shroud of Turin, which he worked on in person. Many people believe it's the burial cloth of Jesus. He even hanged one of his sons on a cross to prove Christ did not die of asphyxiation as many believed. Dr. Zugibe was thorough and his quotes were graphic.

"The attack on the Sohns was the most savage I've ever investigated. Arnold Sohn's skull was shattered like an eggshell. His upper and lower teeth were knocked out. His right thumb was almost totally severed. Other fingers were broken, meaning he may have tried to ward off blows from his attacker.

"Elaine Sohn may have fainted before she was dragged into the bathtub where she drowned. I reached that conclusion because she weighed two hundred pounds. She didn't have a mark on her."

Ken Gribetz was usually an outstanding source. He was

a mover and shaker of every law enforcement department in Rockland County. He was a thin, wiry man of around forty. People who worked out at his gym said despite his size, he was the strongest one there. He talked in a staccato. He didn't like going on tape for radio but didn't shy away from television cameras.

He was always in the know. I realized he had a homicide to solve. If he gave out too much information, his suspect may flee. Some of the evidence may be compromised. He'd be accused of trying his case in the media. He only trusted a few reporters. Fortunately, I was one of them.

I called him at his home.

He said some of the evidence was ruined because the water was left running in the bathtub where Elaine Sohn died.

"When I got there, water was pouring down the stairs like a waterfall. It damaged the bathroom, bedroom, and the rooms downstairs.

"The house wasn't ransacked. Some jewelry is missing."

"Any ideas?"

"You didn't get any of this from me . . . off the record, OK? Sheryl Sohn may be involved at some level. We're looking for a couple of Tobey's. Don't use that yet. We believe there were two people who did this."

The "on the record" stuff was a rehash of the case, along with the usual line about how all the law enforcement people are cooperating on this one. Cops from different departments rarely cooperated with each other. When they did, it was always mentioned.

I called Spring Valley police again and got the short straw, Lieutenant Paul Toth.

"I believe in the Soviet style of news management," he once told me. "The government decides what the public needs to know. That way, you news pukes don't get to fuck everything up."

He put Chief Krainiak on the phone.

"I heard more than one person was involved. Is that true?"

He's willing to go on tape.

"I would think by the size of the two victims that it would appear likely that more than one participant had to do with this particular crime. The female victim weighed over two hundred pounds. Our detectives are working full time on it, and they have conducted many interviews, and we have nothing further to report."

"Any suspects yet?"

"I can't say."

So I can go with "more than one."

Krainiak continued with a non-answer, "Anyone who may have information, no matter how trivial they may feel it is, if they could call us we would treat the call with the strictest confidentiality. We've had some phone calls. *Minimal.* They're giving us indications of some things which we have been checking on."

Lieutenant Toth got back on the phone.

"Sheryl Sohn is undergoing some intensive questioning about her friends. She's dazed and in shock. Her brother just flew in from Florida. He hasn't spoken to us yet."

I wouldn't even imply Sheryl may be a suspect when I wrote my stories.

I made that mistake about a year ago. Police told me a young woman working at a bank in Spring Valley had disappeared with over forty thousand dollars. They led me to believe she stole the money, and that's how I reported it.

Her mother called me at the radio station in tears, asking how I could do something like that.

"My daughter was perfect. She was a good girl who never stole a thing."

I offered to let her go on tape to tell her daughter's side of the story.

"The damage is done already," she sobbed.

Several weeks later, her daughter's bound and gagged body was found floating in the Hudson River near 79th Street in New York City.

Some stories you can't take back.

I needed more stuff for the morning. I left a boring voicer on people complaining about the inaccuracy of the 1980 census.

Our afternoon guy, Dave Peters, left one for the AM on how the American auto industry is shaping up against foreign imports. It was sort of local since we had the recently closed Mahwah Ford plant a few miles from here, and the General Motors plant was just across the Hudson River in North Tarrytown.

December 30, 1980

When I got to work, I found out police said at least two people were being sought for questioning only. They were giving out more information. They said three open bottles of liquor were found along with two glasses in the bedroom of the Sohn home. A ten-thousand-dollar ring along with other jewelry and gold chains were missing. The total loss was about thirty-five thousand dollars.

There was a long tape recording I had to cut up from a phone conversation one of the reporters had with Dr. Zugibe. It was pretty much what we had already, only more formal.

"We found the cause of death of Elaine Sohn to be drowning, which was, of course, in the bathtub. The cause of death in the case of Arnold Sohn was severe injury to the head and brain due to blows from a blunt instrument of sorts. He also had stab marks to the head region. Most of the severe injuries were done with some type of a real hard blunt instrument which totally damaged his skull and brain. Both literally destroyed the entire head. It's one of the most brutal cases we've ever had in the county."

Five

This May Be Your Lucky Day!

Working at WRKL-AM was so different than my afternoon job at WRNW-FM. This was the radio station I listened to religiously when I moved to Rockland County. It was a throwback progressive rock station. The jocks were allowed by program director Gary Axelbank to play virtually anything they wanted on the massive playlist. This was how FM radio was built in the late 1960s. Most eventually became corporate and boring with limited playlists and overly polished sounding disk jockeys.

Where else but at WRNW could you hear Jona Lewie's "You Can Always Find Him in the Kitchen at Parties" along with the Mark Almond Band's version of "New York State of Mind" and "Getaway" from the Rossington Collins Band?

It was a springboard for some who had been there very recently. They included people like Howard Stern, Meg

Griffin, and her husband, Joe from Chicago who moved to WPIX-FM, Earle Bailey to WNEW-FM, and Al Bernstein to WYNY-FM.

When I got there, the big names were Curtis Kaye, Gary Axelbank, Bruce Figler, Donna Donna, and Ray Haneski. All were musically highly knowledgeable.

Unlike WRKL where news was king, it was music that steered the ship at WRNW. Axelbank doubled as the afternoon jock. He also did a show called "Spotlight 107" where hot local talent got an hour to show what they can do. It was local music radio at its best.

Looking back, I sent a tape and resume to WRNW sometime in January 1980. I heard nothing, so I forgot about it. That wasn't unusual. I usually followed up with a phone call or two, but this job seemed too far-fetched for me.

I got a call in mid-summer.

"If you're Bob LeMoullec, this is your lucky day. I'm Gary Axelbank. Are you still interested in working here?"

They had an opening for their afternoon news slot. This was a four-hour gig, Monday through Friday, from two to six. It entailed ripping the wire and reading about one or two minutes of news at the top and bottom of the hour.

The length of the casts weren't etched in stone. I could be done shortly after six and on the road by quarter after. That would give me plenty of time to get to WRKL by seven.

I immediately shit, showered, and shaved. I hopped in my car and headed to Briarcliff Manor.

At first, I wasn't sure I was in the right place. The radio station was in an old, dilapidated one-family house behind a strip mall. It looked like a frat house. It had the same look on the inside. Papers were strewn about. Posters of rock stars were plastered on the walls. Half-empty soda cans were on the desks. A bunch of grungy, disheveled people were sitting around.

The offices were downstairs. The on-air and production studios were on the second floor. There was no newsroom; just a news corner. There were no tape recorders or cart machines, just an old Smith-Corona typewriter on a small stand with a folding chair in front of it. At least the typewriter was electric.

There's one thing I'd say about radio stations, and this went for WRKL as well.

Most of the people who worked there look like clients at a homeless shelter.

In fact, most of the people who worked in the business were a short step away from being homeless.

What kept us going was the love of the job combined with the strong belief we'd find *la dolce vita* someday. It was no secret, people like me who worked in radio had "radio faces." If you were good-looking, you headed for television.

Thus, the down-and-out, disheveled look became a style statement of sorts. Of course, when you left the station to cover a meeting or news conference, you had to look presentable. The exceptions were camera people who never looked dressed for success.

I think I got the job at WRKL because I wore a jacket and tie to the interview. I had to audition for this job.

Gary set me up in a production studio, which was basically a room with a board and some recording equipment. He gave me a couple of pieces of news copy. I read into a reel-to-reel recorder and dubbed it onto a cart.

I handed it to Gary. We listened to it together.

"That's great! When can you start?"

He was very gracious. He walked around the second floor where the studios were with the cart saying to no one in particular, "You've got to hear this, it's great."

I got Gary to get me a reel-to-reel, a cart machine, and a phone line so I could do more than rip and read. There was one hitch: I couldn't use my name at WRNW. Gary thought it would cheapen the air product, so to speak, if listeners thought I worked at more than one place.

"Our traffic reporter is Jay O'Brian. He also goes by Joe Nolan on other stations." We discussed it, and I ended up being called Newsman Bob L on the air.

Debbie Nigro was the news director. She had virtually no news experience. Talk would be her forte. She was extremely bright and personable and was cool with the changes. I tried to do stories at WRNW that were more personality oriented. At WRKL, the listeners wanted to know about that new street light going up on Route 202. At WRNW, the news was somewhat of a nuisance to the listener who just wanted great music and outstanding DJs, so I tried to make it more issue oriented and entertaining.

The Sohn murders had no place at a progressive rock station, especially across the river in Westchester. On the other hand, stories about the Indian Point nuclear power plants in northern Westchester County did. As I mentioned before, everyone remembered the partial meltdown at Three Mile Island not long ago.

An autopsy was scheduled today in the wake of singer Tim Hardin's death. It's common knowledge he was a morphine and heroin addict. It was a story we could use at both radio stations. He was only thirty-nine. WRNW would play his "Reason to Believe" and "If I was a Carpenter." WRKL might have a copy of the latter by Bobby Darin. We'd see.

Six

Not a Radio Face, Far From It

I mentioned "radio faces." There was one notable exception at WRKL. Eti was an intern. She breezed in like something rarely seen in a radio newsroom. Her long shiny brownish-blonde hair draped almost to her thin waist. Her blue eyes, perfect nose, and smooth milk skin were portrait perfect. Her smile could take your breath away. You didn't talk to Eti. No one did. You secretly admired her from a distance. Everyone did.

There are fantasies, and there's reality. The Eti fantasy is I'm looking at an oasis in the middle of a desert. The reality is I'm part of that desert. Eti told some people I reminded her of Charles Manson. How about another reality check? She was twenty, and I was thirty-four.

The great sportswriter, Jimmy Cannon, had it best when he wrote something like: "You don't buy fish on sale, don't bet against the Yankees in October, and pretty young things never fall for older men who aren't rich." Maybe he didn't say it in that order, but you get the picture.

He was wrong. You can always put curry on fish, the Yankees are no longer locks for championships, and love works in strange ways. Truth be told, Eti seduced me. I was sort of a health food nut, so she bought me carob candy bars. I drank about ten cups of coffee a night to stay awake, and she always had coffee brewed for me. I ate frozen blintzes, so she brought me these incredible fresh blintzes her mother made. I acquired a taste for Mother's gefilte fish in a jar, which I ate once in awhile. Eti brought me homemade gefilte fish. She laughed at my shitty jokes.

She started interning in May but didn't start working my shift until about five months later. When she first saw me, I was sleeping on the faux leather couch in the main office. It was around midnight, and I was between jobs. Our maintenance man, Wally Schweitzer, said, "Stay away from him, he's trouble." I still don't know why he said that. I really kept my eye on her since early November when she and a girlfriend visited me at WRNW. They went to Pace University just up the road in Pleasantville.

Eti later told me the two sat in the car in the parking lot and screamed with laughter as they were leaving the station. By Thanksgiving, I was reminding myself of a Hot Tuna lyric: "There I found myself with you, and breathing felt like something new."

We played Frisbee in the WRKL parking lot that night. I guess we were an item at the WRKL Holiday party on December fifth. A week later, the Bear Mountain Inn had its Santa Claus arrival celebration. This was the kind of local story WRKL thrived on.

I told Eti she could cover it, and I'd go along to show her how it's done.

Bear Mountain was an idyllic setting for the winter holidays. Outside, it was bitter cold. Inside, there was a roaring fireplace. A large gingerbread house sat in the middle of the huge room that was decorated for the holidays. Everyone was in a festive mood. Especially Santa! He couldn't stand up straight. Old St. Nick was reeking of alcohol. His potent breath hid the body odor that osmosed from under his threadbare red suit.

Eti sat on Santa's lap with her microphone and tape recorder. She thought he had a load in his pants. After the "interview," we headed to the bar where I ordered two Irish coffees. Unbeknownst to me, Eti didn't drink. Not alcohol. Not coffee. She courageously downed the strong bitter swill without complaining.

We kissed. Fireworks went off. The rest would be history.

When she got home, she woke her mother and told her she's getting married.

"To who?"

"Bob."

"Your boss? The one you said we should suspect if you went missing? Go to sleep and we'll talk about it in the morning."

The following week, I met her parents. It was her mother's forty-third birthday party, and dozens of people were at their beautiful house in Monsey. Lt. Paul Toth was there. It turned out he was a friend of Eti's family.

Eti was stunning in a gold-topped blouse and black

form-fitting pants. Her light brown hair draped about seven inches off her thin shoulders.

Even I was a bit dressed up, if you call a teal blue shirt and a tan sweater that had a collar and brown pants dressy.

There was a wet bar in the corner of the basement where the party was held. I tended bar, which gave me an informal chance to meet and greet virtually everyone.

It's a good feeling when you know someone loves you.

Eti said to her grandmother, "Here's the boy I told you I'm going out with."

Baba didn't look happy. "That's not a boy, that's a man."

December 31, 1980

The Shaarey Tfiloah synagogue was packed for the funeral of Arnold and Elaine Sohn. It seemed as if every politician in Rockland County showed up. Rich Mendelson covered this.

He said Sheryl and Mark Sohn appeared somber as they followed their parents' caskets from the synagogue. It was a bitter cold afternoon.

"Sheryl seemed to have an entourage of police officers around her. I don't know. She seemed pretty stoic." Only Mark was crying. "We were all freezing our asses off. Some of the people there complained about the overwhelming media coverage."

I bet it was the media that brought most of these "friends" out. The cops also complained the media interest made the investigation more difficult.

In the meantime, *Dr. Strangelove* came to Nyack in the form of a fluoridation fight. You may remember the Sterling Hayden character from the movie, General Jack D. Ripper. General Jack said fluoridation was a commie plot to poison all of us.

One of the village trustees who resembled Hayden in appearance and in speech was fighting to keep fluorides out of Nyack's water supply. The county health department threatened to levy a "five hundred dollar a day" fine if the village failed to comply.

I got three sound bites from him as well as from the health commissioner. In the newsroom, Donna Summers's "I Feel Love" came out on the speakers. How did that sneak through?

Tonight, Eti would meet my brother and sister and their significant others. My brother, Elliott and his wife Ruth lived in Rockland County. They held a New Year's Eve party every year. My sister, Genie, and her husband, Sal, were there.

Genie was one year younger than I. Elliott was two years younger. I was sure they'd have something to say later about my bringing a twenty-year-old to the party. A beautiful twenty-year-old at that!

Ruth told Eti in a moment of indiscretion, "Bob always brings beautiful girls to our parties." I'd hear about this later, that was for sure.

Seven

Top of My Game

January 1, 1981

Big things would be in store for me this year. I just knew it. I planned to rework my resume and cover letter. My dream job was someplace like all news radio stations 1010 WINS or WCBS, or top-notch operations such as WNEW or WOR. That seemed out of reach at this point. It was too big a jump from the minor leagues, but I could dream.

It didn't hurt that I gained invaluable experience and knowledge at a premiere shop. The perception was if you worked in a small market, you weren't as good as those in the majors. The reality was very different. Radio is the perception business.

I truly felt I was at the top of my game.

Plan A would be to try for some of the lesser news departments in New York City. It was time I made a living at this. Maybe someone would bite. It was frustrating to think you know pretty much all you need to know to move up, and no one gave you a sniff.

"I'm goin' nowhere . . . somebody help me . . . somebody help me, yeah" is blaring from the speaker. I could relate to "Staying Alive" by the Bee Gees. That was for sure. It was a big leap to go from a mediocre at best disc jockey to an important player in a highly respected news department like WRKL.

I got there mainly through the kindness of co-workers and friends. I'd get sent to a village or town board meeting and would be totally lost until someone like Dave Colton, Will David, or James Walsh from the *Journal News* would say, "That's your lead," or "do it this way."

I picked up that part of it soon enough. The key to success in news was being interested and paying attention to what's going on between the lines.

The writing was a bit tougher.

I had a style that would work for the *New York Times*. That was the complete opposite of broadcast writing which was to say if it sounded like writing, you were off the track.

Rich Mendelson was on the night desk then. I'd take forever to write a story, as if each one had to win a Peabody before I was satisfied.

"You know, Bob, I couldn't send you to cover a fire. By the time your story was written, construction crews would already be on the site rebuilding the place."

Then there were the amateurisms, like not putting the lead in the first sentence. Crap like "the Haverstraw town board met last night" is boring and dated. How about leading with the name of a person no one outside of their family and friends ever heard of? Don't do it. Leading with a question was another faux pas. So were "good news, bad news" leads. Don't use words like *continues* in a lead. Translated, that means nothing is happening.

Mendelson was extremely patient. There were times I'd hand him my copy, and he'd put his head down on the desk and make believe he was crying. He'd say, "Your sentences have to be shorter. I want one subject per sentence. That's it."

Words like *blaze* instead of *fire* were out. There were dozens of those newspaper words that don't work in radio.

"Be accurate. They're Canada geese, not Canadian geese. If they were Canadian geese, they'd need a green card." "Use synonyms freely."

I can tell you first-hand that synonyms also have to be accurate. When I was in the navy, we were ordered to go to Vietnam. This made it more important that everyone get updated dog tags. I got the short straw, so it became my job to type all the information on the two rounded metal rectangles we wore around our necks. Names, service numbers, blood types and religions were included on the tags. Those with no religion would say "none." Some told me Catholic, others Protestant, Jewish, no preference, or none. To save time, I made all non-religious, "none."

When I got back to the ship, all was well until a Chief Petty Officer started screaming, "I thought I told you no preference. *None*! What the fuck is *none*?"

"What's the difference?" I looked over at him standing angrily next to the bulkhead.

"I don't see it. Is it like atheist and agnostic? I know one doesn't believe in God at all, and the other wants evidence first."

The thought of redoing his dog tag for no reason didn't turn me on. He was really pissed.

"When it comes to pussy, there's a big difference between no preference and none."

January 2, 1981

I was sitting in the WRKL newsroom looking around this dreary dump on the edge of a swamp in the northern hinterland of Rockland County. I mentioned WRNW had posters of rock bands on its walls. With one exception, the walls of the WRKL newsroom were covered with old copy that had to be followed up, memos from Bob Marvin, assignments, and on occasion, dollar bills. If someone owed someone else money, there would be no problem taping a few bills to the wall with a note. Money was never stolen.

Now food was another matter. You couldn't leave your food in the refrigerator. It wouldn't survive into the next shift. It would be nothing to see a reporter scrounging through the fridge, asking, "Is any of this yours?"

At one time, one of our reporters was nursing. She pumped her milk at work and left it in the refrigerator. One staffer put it in her tea. Who knew? Happily, I drank my coffee black.

I brought the only poster in the newsroom. It was from the Whispers' new album, "Minimum Wage Rock and Roll." The title described local radio to a T.

Here was an insight into how my mind kept working: I blacked out the "Whi" from the Whispers, and with the back of an eraser, I changed the last s to an m. Now it was "the Sperm." It got enough laughs that no one took it down.

The newsroom was far from "state of the art," considering how many stories we generated. In fact, everything seemed to be patched together. It was a narrow space that ran the length of the building. We had two old reel-to-reel recorders in the front and a third at a station in the rear. They were patched into mixers that hooked into cart machines and very old telephones that allowed us to listen to and record on one of the five lines.

The tapes were cut into sound bites and downloaded onto the carts. The carts were numbered. There was a Braille strip on each one so Steve Possell, a blind disk jockey, could "read" it like the rest of us during the newscast. These numbers were also written on corresponding copy so the correct actuality would be used. The erased carts were kept on racks hooked into the concrete block wall.

There were two bulk erasers. They were electromagnets that were used to erase the carts, so they could be reused. Reel to reels automatically erased tapes as you recorded over them. Cart machines didn't do that. It was important that carts were completely erased; otherwise you'd hear strange woofing noises in the background as they were played on the air.

We had five Smith-Corona electric typewriters. None of them worked too well. The main problem was the letters weren't always aligned. Sometimes they skipped a space. It didn't matter much because the copy, after it was done, had black lines in marker crossed over it in several places in lieu of whiting out corrections. Extra phrases were handwritten over other sentences.

There was a long black table running along the narrow newsroom. That was where the copy with the carts was placed when they were ready for air. We needed a long table for all the stories we did.

The copy was written in triplicate. There was a white copy, a pink copy, and a yellow one. The white went on the table with the carts. The pink was filed by date, and the yellow by subject. Everybody did the filing.

You could enter the newsroom from the main offices or from the pockmarked parking area on the side of the building. That was the entrance of choice. There apparently was no money for fixing the lot, so you had to drive through it like you're riding a bronco. There was a huge swamp in the back where our two towers were situated.

When you came in from the outside, you'd find our Associated Press teletype machine on the right. This machine chattered out news copy from around the world as well as locally. The local stories generally came from us. The AP gave each of us about forty dollars every three months in exchange for calling in stories it used.

Every little bit helped. The worst part about the teletype machine was someone had to change the ribbon. This meant getting ink all over your fingers and subsequently your clothes. The news copy got to be so light that it was virtually unreadable before someone broke down and volunteered to change the ribbon.

This was another reason everyone dressed like shit, unless you knew you were going out to cover a story. The paper came in boxes. The long reams were attached like toilet paper. It simply ran through the back of the machine. A red stripe showed up when the paper was about to run out. It was easy and had to be done. Otherwise, there would be nothing on the world and national wire to read when the anchor came in at five in the morning.

I wondered what the world was coming to. The publishers of *Consumer Reports* announced huge layoffs. It planned to shut down one of its plants here in Rockland County. That meant one hundred seventy workers would be put on the street. Talk about an image problem.

Consumer Union was based in Westchester. The Rockland center handled data processing, printing, and other functions. The company said it costs about one and a half million dollars a year to run.

In the spirit of consumer advocacy, or whatever, the company said it would give the laid-off workers a substantial severance package along with job training and other benefits it worked out with the Newspaper Guild.

The work done at the plant would be given to independent contractors.

I told Eti, I'd take her to the Chateau Blanc for dinner that night. She'd find out soon enough that's French for White Castle.

January 3, 1981

Our local state senator, Linda Winikow, was in full glory. I was told she was the most powerful woman in Albany. So when she had her gall bladder removed, it was an event. Winikow was a heavy-set woman with hair graying at the temples. She was very vocal, to say the least.

She was at Nyack Hospital. It was probably no coincidence that the hospital's three hundred nurses had just made a deal with management on a new contract. They had been threatening to walk out.

Linda called me and spent a half hour describing the operation and its post-operative effects.

"I got a visit from Ed Koch. He even sat on my bed."

I told her I was rolling tape as she spoke. She nearly died.

I tried to imagine Winikow and the New York City mayor. Not a bad rumor to get started.

Never trust anyone in real estate.

The real estate lady who got an apartment for me back in March told me it had a view of the Hudson River. Sure it did, if you stood on the toilet and stuck your head about a foot out of the bathroom window.

Then you could see the Tappan Zee Bridge and the General Motors plant in North Tarrytown. That's where the Stanley Steamers were made in the 1890s. Forget about nostalgia. Workers there hoped GM wouldn't close the plant as Ford did in nearby Mahwah, New Jersey, last summer. There were hints they might.

The apartment was pretty small. There were three rooms in a space about twenty-five feet by twenty-five feet. The kitchen was about the tiniest I ever saw, and I had lived in New York City.

If I had a PTA mom's ass, I couldn't fit in there. My Formica dining room table was in the living room. I had about three hundred record albums set up in wooden fruit crates on the other side. My bookshelves were chipboard with real wood-looking veneer. I also had a black convertible couch.

The bedroom wasn't anything to speak of either. There was room for a small bed and a chest. I kept the place very neat. That was the key. If it was neat and clean, you felt richer.

I was in a nice neighborhood. South Nyack was made up of mostly large colonial homes built way before the turn of the century. Sometimes I saw Helen Hayes when I went walking. She lived down the block. I'll admit to being a bit star struck.

I remember working with her on a public service announcement a few months back. Miss Hayes came into the WRKL production studio with an entourage of a few ladies her age. Everyone doted over her as she tried several times to perfectly get through the script. It took several takes.

I attended her eightieth birthday party in October. Not as a guest, mind you. I mentioned the PSA to her. She acted as if she vaguely remembered.

We reporters got to horn in on big events where we could eat free food in exchange for free publicity. When you were there, you forgot the financial gap between us and them is monumental.

I should have headlined my story, "FREELOADING AT A GARDEN PARTY." We mainly hobnobbed with our journalistic counterparts.

Bunny Crumpacker was there, freelancing for the *Journal News*. Her day job was spokeswoman for the Nyack School District. She's one of the few spokespeople you could trust not to burn you on a good story if one was there. I think I was partly responsible for Bunny getting that job.

A year and a half ago, I did an investigative documentary on how the district got ripped off by builders working on their new field house. A few dads running a private football program called the Nyack Indians complained to me the work seemed shoddy, the lockers were too small to hold the equipment, etc., etc.

I got them to complain into my tape recorder. I brought in a respected builder who told me he could have done the job for less than half the price.

Almost every school district has a board member who beats to a different drum. In Nyack, it was Paul Giacobbe. I got him on tape complaining about the waste of money.

Our news director at the time said it was financed with federal money, so he called the FBI and asked them to investigate. That way we could do a story leading with "the FBI is investigating . . . "

The school board president resigned, I won an award from the Associated Press, the football dads were told they could no longer use the lockers and facilities they complained about, and the district decided it needed a spokesperson—so they hired Bunny.

Back to the party. It had a name: Victorian Garden Party. It doubled as a fund-raiser to preserve the Tappan Zee Playhouse. This was a dilapidated vaudeville house that also showed the earliest movies dating back to 1911. Helen Hayes acted there, as did a number of other household names of the day.

Actress Arlene Dahl and her boyfriend, Marc Rosen hosted the party at their home which was called Treetops. He had something to do with cosmetics, which was good for her. She was about thirty years older than him but looked much younger thanks to whatever he was selling.

The house was built sometime in the mid-1850s. For twenty-five bucks, the riff raff got to hang around luminaries that included Ellen Burstyn, Joan Fontaine, Celeste Holm,

Maureen O'Sullivan, Ann Jackson, and Eli Wallach among others. About four hundred bought tickets.

The female stars were dressed in antique lace and carried parasols. The men wore top hats. The fund-raiser was a losing proposition. More money was spent on the party than what they raised. I was told all their fund-raisers lost money.

The bottom line is a good time was had by all, and I was well fed for a change.

I'd eat the fish dicks tomorrow.

January 4, 1981

Remember the hostages being held in Iran? You know the ones who cost Jimmy Carter his presidency. Well, president-elect Ronald Reagan and his cronies decided to show some teeth. He wasn't in office yet, and already he said he had an action list that included military strikes against the "barbarians." He also apparently got old warmonger Henry Kissinger to say an invasion of Iran wasn't out of the question.

That got a response, all right. Tehran leaders moved all fifty-two of the hostages to undisclosed locations.

Meanwhile, the Sohn case was on the back burner. We were reduced to calling hardware stores to see if people were buying locks or alarms for their homes. The paper did that story a few days ago.

January 5, 1981

Bob Marvin just read the riot act to our weatherman, Mark Hanok. Everyone else in the New York media was predicting up to eighteen inches of snow. Mark says it wouldn't be more than six inches.

It was about ratings. Not that we had any.

New York City media always beefed up their forecasts to scare listeners or viewers into tuning in.

This was the same Bob Marvin who insisted we don't do traffic reports. They were provided gratis by Shadow in exchange for playing their commercials on our air. It's not like we were jam-packed with spots.

Marvin knew dire predictions built audiences.

Mark told me Marvin screamed at him, "You're telling the listener to go somewhere else with your usual weak forecasts."

January 6, 1981

Six inches of snow fell overnight. Six inches isn't much, but it was enough to close schools and just about everything else humans do. It also meant on-air reading through hundreds of closings over and over again. That was what the so-called lucky disk jockeys were stuck doing.

For the rest of us, it meant hitting the road for "lifestyle" reports. You know the drill: kids playing in the snow, mailmen going through the rounds, coffee sales at the 7-Eleven, and how the guys driving the plows are doing. Then we had outages, accidents, and disabled cars.

I drove to WRNW in this. After six, I returned to WRKL for my shift. I loved snow.

Today was my father's birthday. He turned fifty-six. Almost no one on his side of the family got past fifty-nine, so he didn't celebrate these things.

January 7, 1981

My politics skewed to the left. You'd never know it by listening to my copy. What I wrote was always fair. I did tend to put some stories on the air that leant toward my point of view.

Luckily, Lori Siegel volunteered to go all the way to Manhattan to cover the anti-draft rally that took place outside the General Post Office on Eighth and Thirty-third. Lori said there were numerous arrests of demonstrators who refused to move.

"There were plenty of 'hell no, we won't go' chants coupled with signs that included 'give them a draft and they'll give you a war.'"

Nearly two million men born in 1963 were required to register for the draft starting this week. This wasn't President-elect Reagan's fault. We knew he was a cold warrior. The feeling was it was only a matter of time before he became empowered to send our guys overseas on some anti-communist crusade or other adventure.

Most of the protestors were teenagers. What better way to radicalize young people than to threaten them with military service.

Meanwhile, the nuke plant across the river reared its ugly head again. A few months ago, one hundred thousand gallons of water leaked from the system that was supposed to cool the nuclear fuel rods into the Hudson River. Instead, the water ended up heating thousands of fish.

The plant shutdown cost the utility eight hundred thousand dollars a day. Instead of charging the stockholders, Con Ed stuck a 10 percent surcharge on their customers' electric bills.

Not everyone went along.

Con Ed went after about one hundred people who with-held 10 percent of their bills. The utility said the grand loss to their treasury was two hundred seventy-five dollars a month. It cost them thousands to sue. Con Ed's rationale was if one hundred customers could get away with it, anyone could.

With all the leaks, you'd think there'd be a workable evacuation plan. Three Mile Island was still on many minds.

There were about twenty-five million of us living within a fifty-mile radius of the plants. There were three. Con Ed owned one, and the New York State Power Authority owned the other two. The oldest of these was shut.

I needed more stories for the morning. I sent Eti to cover the Nyack School Board. There was talk of building a new high school. I told her to get with Bunny Crumpacker and/or Paul Giacobbe. They'd steer her straight.

We received our weekly taped "news rundown" from local congressman Ben Gilman .No self-respecting operation should put audio news releases on the air. Not really. On the other hand, we had hours and hours of time to fill every day.

We were selective because we didn't want to do any politician's bidding. One thing about Ben: he loved his trim. His ex accused the congressman in divorce papers of having numerous affairs and fathering a child out of wedlock.

When Gilman was interesting, we'd cut out a few sound bites and make it seem like we spoke to him over the phone. The problem with Gilman is he sounded like a programmed robot. I'd bet no one who ever listened to a newscast would believe this was an actual interview.

We've tried to solve the problem by running his studio quality tape through the phone. That gave it a rougher sound. The best I could say about this was he sent his tapes in unmarked boxes. We used them to send out our own air checks. For this, we'd like to thank the congressman and the taxpaying public.

You didn't hear a police chief say very often he'd been duped. Frank Dailey was Sloatsburg's top cop. He wouldn't be for long.

I got an angry call from him. It was to send a message to his bosses. "I lost big money to become a glorified traffic cop. I didn't realize I'd be taking orders from board members whose knowledge of police work comes from 'Kojak.' I was promised more money plus moving expenses."

Dailey was a vice squad detective in New York City before coming to Rockland. I guess it'll be back to chasing pimps, prostitutes, and druggies for him.

Evan Weiner was the top reporter at WGRC. He also called me at the station. "Who's that beautiful girl you sent to Nyack? Is she single?"

"Yes, Eti is single, but forget about it. We don't have a chance. She only goes for blond beach boys with Noxzema on their noses."

January 9, 1981

Again, off the record, I was told Sheryl Sohn was at the center of the investigation into the murders of her parents.

I had to rewarm this story since nothing seemed to be happening.

Lieutenant Paul Toth confirmed the tip for me. "We're looking for two suspects. Sheryl has hired a lawyer. That's as far as I can go."

I put the story on the air. That gave us a new lead along with new information. I beefed it up with a rehash for those who had been out of town or who just forgot. The basic format for updating any news story is new stuff, even if it's only one sentence, followed by rehash.

A worker was exposed to radiation at one of the Indian Point plants. The Nuclear Regulatory Commission seemed to be doing the public relations on this one. The agency said the employee isn't in danger. Get this, "He just used up his quarterly allotment."

The NRC said a radiologist is allowed three rems of radiation per quarter under federal guidelines. A rem is a unit of radiation absorbed in living tissue.

Leaving WRNW, I noticed Debbie Nigro left a note on the follow sheet, "Have an erotic weekend." Thanks, Deb. I saw it as "Turning Japanese" by the Vapors was coming out of the speakers.

WRNW did a weekly show Fridays from the Left Bank in Mount Vernon. This was a hot rock club that mainly showcased local talent. There were some up-and-comers as well.

Joan Jett and the Blackhearts were scheduled to play the following day. R.E.M. was on the calendar. They were to release their first single soon.

I took the latest love of my life and two of her friends,

Toby and Loren, to see Chris Spedding. There was a long line waiting at the door. We walked right in. At WRKL, this never happened. There, we played nothing but old songs. That translated into no perks from the record companies. On the other hand, the politicians kept us fed while we freeloaded at their fund-raisers.

Spedding was more than a little out there to this trio of Barry Manilow and Barbra Streisand fans. He produced the first Sex Pistols album, to give you an idea. He was mainly a session musician. You probably heard his guitar work on dozens of songs and didn't know it.

Eti's two pals left the show wondering what she saw in me while telling each other it won't last.

January 10, 1981

One of our DJs was crowing about the coup he pulled off. Steve Roy got Bob Marvin to voice a faux commercial for him.

"I told him I was pitching Jack LaLanne for some radio spots, and their people insisted in having a mature voice."

"But, Steve, there are no Jack LaLanne gyms in Rockland."

"Right, but I said they're trying to make inroads."

"So what happened?"

"I got him in the production studio, and I gave him a spot I wrote for the occasion. Now I can break it up and play it under my records when he's home and out of our listening area. It has great stuff like, 'Listen up everybody,' 'be the person you always wanted to be,' 'get in shape,' 'tone up those muscles,' 'touch those toes,' 'stretch those arms and legs,' 'that's right.' The possibilities are endless. I can't wait to put it together."

This was inside stuff, but hilarious nonetheless.

"Good luck," I said as Steve headed to the production studio with a stack of records.

Eight

All Shit, All the Time

January 11, 1981

I couldn't believe the shit that was left for me on the news desk. Nothing but shit, and I had to put a bunch of long newscasts together for the morning. What was this, a fucking holiday?

Not only that, but the workspaces were a mess—with spilled coffee, coffee cups, and crumbs all over the place. I worked with a bunch of fucking slobs. I had to clean it before I could get started.

Dr. Daniel Hyman had a piece on flu season. This was a blue sky piece you can do every year. Hyman was the county health commissioner. He kept his dog's nuts in a formaldehyde jar on his desk. Someday I'd do that story, but not today.

There was to be a blood drive coming up in Pearl River

next Sunday. Get this lead: "Pet owners are warned not to allow their dogs and cats to stay outside too long in the bitter cold weather." Are you shitting me?

I know it wasn't a local story, but couldn't someone at least have left a voicer on Richard Dreyfuss' abortion suit? Some woman in Los Angeles sued the actor for supposedly reneging on a promise to pay medical costs if she had an abortion. She did. He didn't. She wanted two and a half million dollars for her ordeal.

Maybe I was pissed because my car was acting up again. It almost didn't start. I yelled at it and threatened to push it off the Tappan Zee Bridge if it didn't get going. I punched the dashboard. It got going.

Now I was back to freezing my ass off again. That's because I had to leave the newsroom window open so I could keep the battery charging. I contemplated pushing the car into the river. There would be no upside. First, I didn't have comprehensive insurance, so it wouldn't pay to say it was stolen. Second, I was never a fan of insurance fraud. Besides, the car was only worth ten bucks. Anyway, getting caught would have been a real career killer.

Dave Peters came in to do some dubbing. Needless to say, we were both wearing winter coats.

Besides the filing system I described, we dubbed every tape that went on the air to master reels which were kept for posterity. We all did it. Dave volunteered to come in on his own time.

He was a thin guy with sandy hair. He majored in music at Pitt. Dave's real name was Pultz. He had a talk show called the "Pittsburgh Pultz" before he came to WRKL. He told me Pultz was too close to putz . . . which didn't play well in New

York, so he changed it to Peters.

Sometimes we called him Dogs. That's because during a newscast, he got confused while reading a bank robbery story, "The crooks got away with five thousand dogs."

He sat on the corner of my desk. "I'm getting back into clean living. No more cigarettes. No more alcohol. I'm even exercising in the morning."

I responded by getting on the floor and doing fifty push-ups. I may have been the oldest guy in the newsroom, but I hadn't lost it. Not by a long shot.

I thought it was time to buy a lead jock. A second leak in two days was reported at Indian Point. The state power authority spokesman compared it to a medical X-ray.

Nine

A Lawnmower Built for Two

We got company at the radio station. Barrie Lipscomb went into a quiet spot where she spent a couple of hours on the phone in what she thought was a very private conversation. I guess she was just a very pretty fortyish woman taking advantage of women's lib.

One of our engineers who also doubled as a DJ ran to the back of the newsroom.

The phone system was a cheapie. It was set up so you could punch any button and listen to any conversation. This was how we taped our interviews for air.

He listened to Barrie who was talking to her gardener. The speakers were on. I overheard someone who sounded like Ricardo Montalban from Fantasy Island and the Chrysler Cordoba commercials.

"Leave your husband. You said no one makes you feel

the way I do. I can make you very happy."

"No, you can't. He buys me things you can't dream of affording. It's just not practical."

"There's more to life than clothing and jewelry. He can't make you go wild the way I do. You're an untamed animal when we're together."

"What are you going to get me, a lawnmower built for two? I can't."

I shook my head. It was amusing, but really over-the-top wrong to be tapping the phones like this.

The Iran hostage situation may end soon. Stay tuned.

January 12, 1981

Bob Marvin was on the warpath. The veins were popping out of the thick neck that led to his bald head. One of our biggest sponsors, the Coachlight Dinner Theater filed for bankruptcy. It was about a million and a half dollars in debt.

The theater owed WRKL a big chunk of change. Most of the deal was trade or barter. In other words, the Coachlight gave us free tickets in exchange for radio spots.

Most radio stations would give these away in contests, but Bob Marvin didn't believe in that. I'm sure he was afraid no one would call. In reality, you could offer a bag of shit to the tenth caller, and someone would be happy to win it.

Marvin let the sales people give the passes to prospective clients. Apparently, the theater wasn't getting much bang for the tickets from us. Plus, Marvin wasn't above sticking it to these guys.

A couple of years ago, they pissed him off about something, so he did an on air "review" of their "Fiddler on the Roof" production. To my knowledge, he'd never done one before. In what I admit was clever writing, he said this version of "Fiddler" had a waspish feeling.

In his whining drone, he said the play had few notable voices. "It lacked . . . schmaltz." In closing, he panned, "This was as if an old Jewish friend turned up converted to a gentile." I doubt this helped the gate.

Ann Jeffries was scheduled to appear at the Coachlight in the "King and I" in a few days. We'd see if Marvin was up to doing another review.

The wires said actor James Cagney was recovering from a bruised knee he suffered in an auto accident on the Taconic Parkway across the river from Rockland. This was your basic fender bender. Cagney refused treatment. The driver of the other car went through the windshield. Somehow, he suffered only cuts and bruises.

Ten

Camelot Murders Solved

January 14, 1981

Finally!

Sheryl Sohn and two others were charged with murdering her parents. Ken Gribetz made the announcement at a well-attended news conference. "She was taken into custody last night by Spring Valley Police. She'll be arraigned later today. According to the indictment, she left open a rear door and sent two men she met at the Camelot bar to wait for her parents until they returned from a party on December 28.

"Twenty-three-year-old Miss Sohn, twenty-five-year-old Belton Lee Brims, and an unnamed codefendant are each charged with second degree murder by a Rockland Grand Jury in a fourteen-count indictment that was handed up last night.

"Brims is currently being held on an unrelated robbery

charge at the Bergen County Jail in New Jersey.

"The third defendant's name hasn't been released because he's still at large."

According to the law in New York, prosecutors were forbidden to release the name of a defendant if his indictment was still sealed.

We knew it was twenty-three-year-old James Sheffield thanks to his lawyer, Public Defender Peter Branti. Branti had been defending him on a couple of unrelated assault charges. Both cases involved savage beatings.

"Miss Sohn wanted a ten-thousand-dollar ring her mother wore. The other two would get the rest of the jewelry."

The DA went on, "She masterminded it. Another motive was hatred toward the mother. We have her confession. She told us she left the back door of her home opened for her two friends. When she was arrested at her girlfriend's house, she showed no surprise, no remorse, and offered no resistance."

Gribetz told me later that she was surprised. Police didn't want to arrest her earlier because they were afraid Brims would figure she was talking and would flee. She thought she was off the hook for helping investigators.

While we were getting dribs and drabs of information from day one, police already had her confession. We had to rely on them. They couldn't tell us everything because they were afraid the other two suspects would disappear. We rarely got the whole story.

It turned out Gribetz knew Arnold Sohn because Arnold had come to him for help. Sheryl was a hard drug abuser. Gribetz got her into Phoenix House.

She stole several hundred dollars from the purse of a co-worker to buy drugs. After she left Phoenix House, she began hanging around in the Camelot bar on Main Street in Spring Valley. The Camelot was known as a drug den.

Indian Point remained an ongoing story. Opponents of the nuclear plant thought they had a chance to get it shut. *Keep dreaming.*

The Nuclear Regulatory Commission said it would conduct a safety hearing at some date in the future. There were several groups around Rockland, Westchester, and other counties that wanted to see it closed. It couldn't come too soon for some.

This news came on the heels of yet another radiation leak. This one poured into a steam system. Con Ed and the NRC said the radiation levels released into the Hudson River were extremely minute.

"Infinitesimal amount" was another phrase in the news release along with word that it fell into "about 1 percent of the limit allowed every three months."

Just don't swim near there. Or go fishing.

The scene was set for Sheryl Sohn's first day in court. The Rockland County Courthouse was a rock solid art deco building that gave the appearance that justice would be served there. It was built in the 1930s. Outside, the walls were granite with gold double doors and columns that made it resemble a large bank. Inside, the floors were marble. There were five courtrooms: two on either side and a small room on the first floor near a stairway leading to the basement. The center was wide open with a balcony. There was gold-embossed writing commemorating Rocklanders who were honored for some reason. The law library was in the cellar. The building was usually very active, even on a slow day. Today it was bustling.

The news media was here in force. The locals were represented by us, WRKL, along with WGRC radio and the Rockland *Journal News*. Also, 1010 WINS was here. WCBS sent Fran Schneidau, who had been covering the Jean Harris trial across the river in Westchester. Harris was accused of killing Scarsdale Diet Doctor Herman Tarnower in a jealous rage. It was one of those "trials of the century" that got national coverage. The AP and UPI were also here. So were the *New York Times*, the *Post,* and the *Daily News*. TV channels 2, 4, 5, 7, 9, and 11 were on hand. This was big. It wasn't Scarsdale Diet Doctor big, but it was big.

Besides us, there were the usual retirees and the curious who spent their days at all the good trials. There were court employees hanging around during their breaks.

In other words, it was standing room only for an arraignment that was expected to take only a few minutes.

Sheryl Sohn's entry into the packed courtroom had a strange feel to it. It reminded me of the Charles Laughton movie, *Hunchback of Notre Dame*, where a contrite Quasimodo was led before the curiosity seekers to the whipping post where he got his.

The handcuffed woman was shielded by a group of correction officers from photographers and cameramen trying to get a good shot. She looked straight ahead as reporters shouted the usual questions, "Did you do it?" "Are you sorry?"

Sohn was silent during the arraignment. She nodded

when County Court Judge Harry Edelstein asked her if she understood the charges against her.

"Yes, I'm aware of them."

Her lawyer, Patrick Burke, spoke. "My client pleads not guilty to the indictment."

He told reporters later, "There's nothing here that shows my client is a murderer. She wasn't there. She may be guilty of something, but it's not murder."

The judge remanded her back to the Rockland County jail while Gribetz and Burke hashed over potential bail in written arguments.

Eleven

Tough Hookers in Detroit and Other Good Stuff

January 15, 1981

Our sports reporter Carl Nathe was staring at the AP wire machine. "How's this for balls. Someone knocked out Leon Spinks and stole his gold teeth."

I was beyond surprised.

"Are you shitting me? Maybe it's not the same Olympic Champ who beat Muhammad Ali for the Heavyweight title. It has to be someone else."

"No, it says here he was leaving a bar in Detroit when someone hit him on the head. When he woke up, he was laying naked in a motel room with forty-five thousand dollars in clothes, jewelry, and teeth gone."

"I'd hate to say it, but they have some tough hookers in

Detroit. I'll remember that the next time I'm there."

"No, you can't say that. Not on the air, anyway. Obviously, the police are looking into it."

"My guess is the champ will be sticking to his story. There's no other way to spin it."

January 16, 1981

A deal to bring the hostages home was apparently finalized. President Carter wanted this done on his watch. All the negotiations took place between representatives from Algeria and Iran. Everything seemed to hinge on transferring frozen Iranian assets to the Tehran government. Reagan's inauguration would be the twentieth. Four days wasn't much time.

Here's a word of advice: If your car isn't inspected, and the registration is expired, it's not a good idea to drive through a toll booth.

The toll taker at the Whitestone Bridge told me to drive to the side, and he called the police officer on duty over. To me, toll takers were just like homeless guys who stick their hands out looking for quarters. Glorified panhandlers!

It was just my luck I got Mister Dedication.

The officer took my license and registration and told me he'd be right back. Ten minutes passed and still no cop. I took off.

I had the other half of my license anyway, and who needed the registration? The one he was holding expired in June.

I told myself it wasn't my fault. My car could never pass an inspection, and you couldn't get your registration renewed without it. Laws were written without poor people in mind.

You'd be glad to know the cost of making a call at a pay phone would remain at ten cents for the foreseeable future. The Public Service Commission turned down a request from the New York Telephone Company to double it to twenty cents.

January 17, 1981

Imagine my shock when I picked up the *Journal News* this morning. It turns out police in North Plainfield, New Jersey, picked up James Sheffield less than seven hours after the Sohn murders. Sheffield was carrying a pillow case containing bloody clothes at the time.

The *Journal News* quoted an officer who said the twenty-three-year-old was held a couple hours because of the bloody clothes and the suspicious way he behaved while he was being questioned.

"He was pacing back and forth as if he was really nervous," Lieutenant Larry Van Winkle told the paper. "I told the fellas he was warming up his sneakers and getting ready to run."

The shocker was they let him go. I guess it wasn't that simple.

According to the paper, he was released after police there checked with Rockland cops and learned there was no warrant for him. There should have been.

That confession from Sheryl Sohn happened the first time they talked to her, the day after the murders. I had no inkling from all the "inside" info I thought I was getting.

So North Plainfield police turned the pillowcase with the bloody clothes to Rockland investigators right after they let Sheffield walk. We called North Plainfield police for some quotes. That way we no longer had to attribute the *Journal News* on the story.

It had to happen sooner or later. My car died on the Sprain Brook Parkway in Westchester. I managed to get the squishy pile of excrement off the road, but it had to be towed to a gas station in Yonkers.

The owner looked like one of those grimy types cast for the Fram Oil Filter "pay me now, or pay me later" commercials.

The mechanic sold me on a ring job I knew I didn't need. What could I do? He had me by the cojones. I can't push the car to Rockland County. At least he said he'd throw in an inspection so the total came in under seventy-five dollars.

Now I could finally get my registration. When I got the bill, I was struck by the forty-two dollar an hour labor charge. *Holy fuck.* I would have been happy making that in one day. It sucked that someone who dropped out of the ninth grade when he turned sixteen could make eight times what I made. My parents always drummed into us that we needed an education in order to make it in this world. Boy, were they wrong.

Mr. Fram Oil Filter tried to hit me with an additional tune-up. He must have thought I had shit between my toes.

January 19, 1981

I had shit between my toes. I should have gotten the tune-up. The bug was still riding rough. There was no way I was going back to Yonkers.

I took an auto repair course at LaGuardia College back in the day. At least now I knew how to do the basics. I went to an auto supply store in Nyack and bought points, four sparkplugs, and a condenser. I already had a gapper for the plugs and a timing light for the belt. The worst part was freezing my ass off, working outside on my car in sub-arctic weather. I really started to hate the cold.

This latest repair should hold me through the rest of the winter.

The hostages, and Jimmy Carter's four-hundred-forty-three-day nightmare, was finally over.

They all began heading home. The hostages would go to Germany first while the president headed there from Washington.

Mendelson scored an interview with local hostage mom Bonnie Graves. Here's what she said:

"I wasn't optimistic before. I didn't get on the roller coaster. Right now, there are technical, practical things that are going on such as all the banks have been busy arranging transfer funds. On the Christmas videotape, my son looked very tired. The Algerians who are brokering the deal said he's in good spirits.

"There's been a superb effort on the part of the Carter administration. They were obviously aided by the Algerians. They've not only resolved the crisis, they reassured the families. They kept a human touch to all this which was very gratifying."

We "balanced" this with so-called Iranian expert David Albert who said America is partly to blame for the hostage situation.

He described atrocities performed by the Shah's regime that he admitted he only read about in the New York Times.

"The CIA gave torture seminars to Iranian officers that were based on German torture techniques. Americans should be aware the Shah's secret police was trained in the United States."

January 20, 1981

Did I say four-hundred-forty-three-day nightmare? Make that four hundred forty-four.

There were apparently too many odds and ends to be cleared up. The bottom line is the Iranians were told if there was no deal while Carter was president, all bets were off, and they'd probably have to deal with Reagan.

We taped Mr. Carter's final speech off the television set. We didn't have an audio news service from the AP or UPI like the big boys. Bob Marvin said that would make us lazy.

Translation: Our sales staff would be forced to sell more ads. *Fat chance of that happening.*

So the deal was made. Reagan became president and that was that. We had no shortage of hostage reaction.

"Iran's frozen assets should be returned, it's their money."

"If Carter had been reelected, this never would have happened."

"I think they were wary of Reagan. If they held on any longer, they might have gotten a more military response from the United States."

"Maybe they're afraid of Reagan."

"You can't be a president and be timid."

Rich Mendelson just got engaged. He brought his bride to be to the station a few times. He definitely overachieved. That was one good thing about radio.

It was like when I tended bar. When you were pouring drinks virtually every girl flirted with you. If you were on the other side of the counter, the same girls would have put their fingers in their mouths and made puking gestures to each other behind your back.

Ted and Joan Kennedy called it quits.

If we could have a divorced president like Reagan, Teddy can end his charade with the minimum of fallout. Joan lived for three years in Boston where she worked on a master's degree in teaching at Leslie College. He lived in Virginia with their children.

One source said they were still good friends.

Bunny Crumpacker did a review of the "King and I" for the *Journal News*. I can't tell whether she loved it or hated it. Our "reviewer" Bob Marvin passed on this one.

January 21, 1981

Paul Toth was named acting chief of the Spring Valley Police Department now that Kraniak left. Kraniak was one good source down the drain in favor of someone who thought we were all a bunch of pussies.

In case I hadn't mentioned it, Eti was a Calvin Klein model not long ago. I told her, just like the Brooke Shields ad, I want to get between her and her Calvin's.

I was trying.

January 23, 1981

We were about to find ourselves in the middle of an international story. The hostages were coming to our area. Congressman Ben Gilman made the announcement live on our air. He still sounded robotic, as if he was on tape. Good for us. Now no one will suspect we use his handouts.

Gilman was the ranking Republican on the House Foreign Affairs Committee. He didn't take credit for the hostages coming into his district.

"This will give the returnees and their families privacy and because of the central location and the proximity to Stewart Airport."

The village of Highland Falls on the banks of the Hudson River sat outside West Point. The normally quiet community bustled with excitement. Yellow ribbons were everywhere. Most were supplied by the local Ben Franklin store.

The owner said he was from New Jersey. He brought up truckloads of anything that's yellow. That included sheets and tablecloths.

A local florist said anything yellow was selling, including ribbons and streamers. Patriotism was in the air. Everybody was in on the act.

Hostage Richard Queen was released from Iran a few months ago when it was learned he had multiple sclerosis. He just finished a public service announcement for the National Multiple Sclerosis Fund to cash in.

"I was an Iranian hostage. Coming home after two hundred fifty days should have been cause for celebration, but for me, the end of one ordeal was the beginning of another. Now I still have to deal with my life threatening illness."

Twelve

You're Not Getting Squab

I decided to splurge and take Eti to dinner and a movie. I saw a coupon in the paper for the Ponderosa. The $5.99 deal was two sirloin strip steak dinners plus an all-you-can-eat salad bar, a baked potato, and a warm roll with butter—all for two people.

I reminded myself of the old joke that the meat still had the whip marks where the jockey hit it. Those salad bars were decent. It came complete with macaroni and cheese, vegetables, and some unidentified fried meat which was probably chicken. At $5.99 for two, you're not getting squab.

The restaurant also threw in a fruit cup, a couple of flavors of Jell-O, and something that was hopefully chocolate pudding.

The Jazz Singer with Neil Diamond and Lucy Arnaz finally made it to one of those buck-fifty movie theaters. The original was better. Not to date myself, but the elementary school I went to in Hempstead, Long Island, often showed old movies for free.

The 1927 Al Jolson version, which was the first talkie, was about a cantor who chose a jazz career over his father's objection. He reconciled at the end with the dying man by singing Kol Nidre on Yom Kippur.

Neil Diamond's was about a cantor/songwriter who dumped his wife and got his new girlfriend pregnant and his father didn't die at the end. Hey, this was the eighties.

Thirteen

Wasted Days and Wasted Nights

January 25, 1981

The hostages were due to land today at nearby Stewart Air Force Base. Then they'd be driven with their families in six buses to West Point where they'd spend the night at the Hotel Thayer.

News director Rich Mendelson had it all planned and well-organized. We were all on the schedule. My shift didn't start until late, but I was scheduled to work much earlier. No one cared that we'd be working practically for free. That's because this really wasn't work, it was a chance to be a part of history.

I looked over my equipment as usual. This wouldn't be the time for excuses. I checked my tape recorder. I grabbed extra batteries and tapes. I had my microphone with the WRKL mike flag. I also had a VoiceAct. The mouthpiece of most pay phones could be screwed off. The VoiceAct could be screwed onto this speaker. It had an input jack that you patched into the output plug on the tape recorder. That way, you could phone the radio station, voice your script, insert the taped actuality, then voice your outro and lockout. An alternative would be to hold the mouthpiece of the phone into the speaker on the tape recorder. The quality wasn't quite the same, and there could be a moment of dead air between your voice and the actuality.

I had some masking tape in case there was a news conference, and I needed to get my microphone hooked up front. I brought a microphone extension cord for the same reason.

A couple of writing pads and non-flair pens, and I was good to go. If you took notes in the rain with a flair pen, you were fucked. Take my word for it. All the ink would smear into an unreadable mess. We learned the hard way to take a ball point pen or a pencil.

I also had a yarmulke in my equipment bag, but I wouldn't need it today.

I drove with Evan Weiner from WGRC north on the scenic part of Route 9W on the west side of the Hudson River. He was supposedly the competition, but at these prices, we pooled our resources.

The first sign of the hostages' homecoming could be seen as soon as you hit the revolutionary war town of Stony Point. There were yellow ribbons on the trees along the way. We saw crowds already gathering by the time we hit Highland Falls.

The hostages would be brought to the village by bus after arriving at Stewart Airport two hours earlier. Flags flapped in the breeze. Red, white, and blue posters proclaimed, "Welcome Home."

Yellow ribbons were on lampposts, buildings, car antennas, and trees. There were dozens of street vendors hoping to make a few bucks on this historic day. Two dollars would get you a small button that read "Free at Last." The cynic in me wondered if these were holdovers from the civil rights era.

Another buck bought you an American flag. I happily found a pay phone and filed a couple of reports. I say *happily* because you never knew where they were and whether one would be available.

The village filled up fast. Cops figured a quarter of a million people would be here when all was said and done. Evan and I got inside West Point. They took us reporters to Stewart Air Force Base by bus.

We heard the state department jet called Freedom One was expected to touch down soon. Families of the former captives had already arrived from Washington on three aircraft.

While we were on the bus, a press flunky announced, "There won't be any interviews of the hostages today."

We were fucked. Now we were hostages since we couldn't get out and make our own arrangements. We didn't get close to the terminal. I found some people who did. I taped quotes from them so I wouldn't be empty-handed when I filed my reports. Some were pretty good.

"My first thought was thank God they're here. It was just a magnificent site to see that plane landing and to see them coming out and meeting their families."

"Incredible, thrilling."

"I tried to send a lot of love their way. I feel the next few weeks are going to be very difficult for them."

At that point, I saw six big shiny green-and-silver buses pass in front of us as they were leaving the airport. It was a stroke of luck that I had something exciting to describe.

A few of the freed hostages looked out in wonder. They smiled and waved through the lightly tinted glass at the masses that surrounded me. I admit I got caught up in the frenzy.

I had a flashback of the time my sister, brother, and I drove a dozen miles on our bicycles to see presidential candidate John Kennedy campaigning at the Bellmore, New York, train station. It was a typically cool October on Long Island. The crowd rushed his motorcade as soon as he arrived. The three of us held our hands over our heads so we wouldn't lose each other in the screaming throng as we were pushed forward. Kennedy looked at us and smiled.

This thrill was right up with that one. I had enough to do my stories.

The bus took Evan and I back to West Point. We headed over to nearby Newburgh to find a pay phone. We wrote our pieces, then did our reports.

Lori Siegel had to put all the reports from the field together in between anchoring her newscasts. Now it was time to head back to our radio stations. I still had to do my shift.

There was no way we could get through Highland Falls now. I knew of a back road that went through West Point.

It was clear.

There was an incredible amount of good stuff on the desk when I got in.

We had tape of ex-hostage Cortlandt Barnes saying, "Instead of 'Tie a Yellow Ribbon Round the Old Oak Tree,' the song should have been Freddy Fender's 'Wasted Days and

Wasted Nights.'" He was with Congressman Gilman who called us.

"We're learning slowly the details of our Americans' captivity. I'm hearing horror stories of threatened firing squads, poor diets, mental abuse, and cruelty. For their bravery and patience, our hostages deserve their nation's gratitude and admiration."

Barnes added, "We're not heroes. The real heroes are the ones who lost their lives trying to rescue us. One day I was doing a job, and the next day I wasn't. We knew we weren't forgotten. We didn't know how unanimous it was, but we knew we weren't forgotten."

A couple of stories on the desk caught my eye.

The Federal Communications Commission in the final days of the Carter administration decided to partially deregulate radio and television. It meant there would no longer be a requirement to have news departments or public affairs programming. My guess was it wouldn't affect me. You could hear the Platters' "The Great Pretender" anywhere, but local news was another story.

Every radio and TV station did news. People needed to know. It shouldn't have an effect.

The FCC also voted to remove the eighteen minutes an hour limit on advertising.

Bob Marvin may feel the pressure down the road, but I doubt it. We never came close to eighteen minutes.

Fourteen

Taxi Twists and Other Turns

The wires also had a story about Dan Rather stiffing a Chicago cabbie. It came down to who you believed. The cab driver said the CBS newscaster refused to pay the fare because his chauffeur's license wasn't displayed. Rather, said the driver kidnapped him and took him on a wild ride along Lake Michigan through Chicago's north side. He claimed his ordeal only ended after a passing motorist noticed him screaming and waving for help.

This story resonated because I drove a yellow cab in New York City for a couple of years.

I'm not a materialist by any stretch. However, the difference between a ten-cent tip and a twenty-five-cent tip could subconsciously make or break your night.

Walter Cronkite gave me thirty-five cents after I drove him a few blocks from his place on Park Avenue. That was average in those days. To his credit, he didn't tell me not to spend it all in one place.

I remember taking this rough-looking character to one of the worst, burned out sections of the south Bronx. It looked like part of World War II was fought there.

There were collapsed and broken buildings plus fenced in lots completely covered with rubble through a wide swath of that part of the borough. Much of the city was like this at the time. I think the Bronx was the worst.

At night, the streets were almost completely deserted. You didn't want to know anyone who hung out there past midnight. If I didn't need the money, I wouldn't have been there either.

I was one of the "liberals" who drove anyone to any place they wanted to go. Gypsy cabs had stickers that read, "We're not yellow. We go anywhere."

It was especially dark. There were no lights. This part of the south Bronx was really desolate. When we pulled up to the nearly abandoned project, my burly fare told me he forgot his wallet.

"Let me get to my apartment where I have the money. I'll be right back."

"Sure," I said as I rolled my eyeballs. "God damn it, I'm not getting stuck," I told myself. "Hold on." I put the cab in park and walked with him into the building.

I had no idea what he was thinking. Probably something like, "This motherfucker is crazy."

There happened to be a woman he knew in the elevator. "I have to pay this guy, do you have any money?" She gave it to him.

He gave me the fare along with a tip. I thanked him and

left.

January 27, 1981

Rich Mendelson got to go to West Point for the ex-hostage news conference. It was one of the perks of being a news director in a small market. He'd sell the sound bites to the Associated Press along with a few radio stations. I bet there was also a generous buffet to satisfy the hungry news types.

Colonel Tom Schaefer was one of the speakers. "In a very short time, we got in two completely different environments. The biggest problem of my day in captivity was trying to determine what I was going to eat with my rice. Forty-eight hours later, President Carter is embracing me with tears in his eyes. I have problems coping with that."

Ex-hostage John Graves said, "The real heroes are the families. We knew what was happening to us. The families did not. We did not experience the roller coaster emotions. We had fourteen months of reading and sleeping and walking five steps, turning and walking another five steps."

Bob Marvin walked into the newsroom as I put the stories together.

"Pretty good, huh?" I asked.

"Adolescent overkill."

January 28, 1981

Steve Roy had to be hands down the funniest person who worked at the radio station.

He also had the most major league sound. He'd never be told to keep it low and slow; he was there already. He also did some sales to supplement his pitiful salary. He and his brother, Jim, stopped over the station with a couple of six packs and a pizza.

Rich Mendelson and I helped them finish everything off. Mendelson was in the building putting together awards packages. Steve told me Eti was his last crush before he got married. I'm sure he wasn't alone. He was pretty upbeat considering Bob Marvin told him he was on probation because he talked too much on the air.

The most professional sounding person talked too much? I guess I heard it all. We think it was that Marvin found out about Steve's high jinks.

Marvin lived out of the radio station's range, so he couldn't hear what Steve did on the air during his weekend show. Steve took advantage of that by pulling hilarious inside stuff.

I mentioned earlier there were several occasions where Steve convinced Marvin to voice commercials for him. The Jack LaLanne spot was only one.

He also used a review of a play at the Coachlight Dinner Theater Marvin did. The word *schmaltz* got heavy airplay.

Here's how it worked: Steve cut out words and phrases of Marvin's whiny voice and injected them into records he played on the air. A disco instrumental was morphed into an exercise tape starring Marvin. One of Steve's favorites was "Get up and Boogie," which wasn't even on the playlist. Playing that may have been a bigger crime.

Isaac Hayes's "Shaft" went something like, "Who is that black private dick that's a sex machine to all the chicks," followed by a pause then a whimpering "Bob Marvin."

That was Bob Marvin's voice that came up where the

word *shaft* should be. You get the picture.

We did have a mishap, thanks to Steve. He dubbed a few hoots from Screaming Jay Hawkins's "I Put a Spell on You" onto a cart. Sometimes in the middle of a record, you'd hear, "Ah ah ah, watch out!"

Steve accidently put the cart where the weather cart usually sat. Our afternoon DJ Steve Possell is blind. He picked up the cart at one point in his show and said, "Now with the weather, here's Mark Hanock." Then the audience heard, "Ah ah ah, watch out!"

Possell jumped a foot in the air. Being the pro that he was, he had a record cued, so he got out of it as best he could. The consensus was our "Garden Hotline" host, Ralph Snodsmith, probably blew the whistle.

It could have been Barrie Lipscomb who mentioned it to Marvin during pillow talk. Who knew? She hated Steve.

Snodsmith was friendly to everyone. The phones for his show lit up even before he got into the building. There was no question the "Garden Hotline" was the most popular program on WRKL.

Ralph had a funny Midwestern or Southern accent. It wouldn't work in New York unless he had something really interesting to talk about. We didn't think he liked Steve, that's why he was a prime suspect.

January 29, 1981

Dave Peters told me I was on the air in Pennsylvania. Tim Scheld who interned for us last year worked at a college station at Saint Francis while he finished his degree in something like business journalism.

Dave sent him some of my hostage stuff, so it was aired at WAMQ near Loretto, Pennsylvania. I didn't even know where that was, but maybe one day I'll put it on my resume.

Most of us were convinced there would be no way twenty-five million people living around Indian Point could get to safety in the event of a meltdown.

Local leaders hoped a few could be saved. They were the ones at the Westchester County Center discussing a rough draft of an evacuation plan. It wouldn't involve everyone, just those within a ten mile radius. We sent Dave Peters.

County Executive Al DelBello weighed in. "It doesn't mean it's practical nor can it be implemented. We're just getting the first serious questions. Are the roads adequate? We have serious doubts."

Others complained a plan would give residents a false sense of security. "They're assuming people who live eleven miles from the plant will just sit there and say they're safe because they're outside the radius."

The NRC said emergency plans must be up and running by April 1. April 1, indeed.

January 30, 1981

I started work at WRNW a few hours early because Debbie Nigro went to the city to cover the ticker tape parade for the former hostages. She didn't file any stories. I guess she wanted to be part of the experience.

When I was there, someone named Joe Renda from Crazy Joe and the Variable Speed Band came in. We chatted for a couple of hours in between my newscasts. He had a record/

music video that started to get some airplay called "Eugene."

It was a novelty song about this obnoxious douche bag played by Joe. I saw the video on a show called "Rock World." It made the WRNW play list. I loved it.

Winter is the best time to be in love. You're warm and bundled inside and out while the bitter wind stings your face.

"Give me something to remember you by, like a kiss on a cold dark night." Well-written, Gary Brooker. I love that song.

I took Eti to see *Altered States*. It was very strange indeed. Remind me never to use those drugs. Not anymore, anyway.

I had taken my fair share of psychedelics back in the day. You know the DuPont slogan, "Better living through chemistry." Now I was pretty straight; hardly any more reefing for me.

The news business was my new addiction.

February 1, 1981

It was the same story, just a different month. Indian Point was leaking again. The only difference from the others was the excuse.

This time, the story was, according to the news release, "apparently a part in one of the three low-pressure turbines at the plant became dislodged, and this resulted in turbine vibration which was noticed by the operators and there were also some condenser leaks.

"So it's surmised that this part also damaged some of the condenser tubes." Got all that?

And the public relations kicker: "All this is located in the non nuclear section of the plant."

We rounded up the usual anti-nuke people for balance. "This is all frightening because you're dealing with a technology that when it goes wrong can have a catastrophic effect."

"The NRC basically does public relations for the press and to assuage our anxiety."

Here was a real good reason to fear radioactivity. Cancer rings that no one warned you about.

A Buffalo woman brought a ring in question to a television station yesterday. She said she bought the ring in 1941. She wore it for six months before she began developing a rash and tumor on her ring finger. She lost the finger in February 1953. Most of her hand was removed about a year later. Then she lost part of her elbow.

Fourteen radioactive contaminated rings surfaced so far in western New York, Pennsylvania, and New York City.

Here's what pissed me off: New York health officials knew of the hazardous rings since 1967. They didn't see fit to make a public warning until the woman went on the air. The gold is believed to come from tiny seeds containing radioactive radon gas used to kill cancerous tumors from the 1930s until the mid-1940s. The seeds somehow ended in the hands of jewelers during that period.

The health department just began urging people with skin problems to have their jewelry checked for radioactivity.

Belton Brims was indicted for robbery in New Jersey. He was also indicted in Rockland for several counts of murder, robbery, and burglary stemming from the Sohn case.

Ken Gribetz commented, "Formal extradition proceedings have been commenced by my office. We sent the appropriate papers to Governor Carey in Albany, and hopefully in a very short period of time, the ball will start rolling that leads to the return of Brims to Rockland County to stand trial.

"It's our understanding that he's refused to waive extradition and will stand trial first in New Jersey on the pending indictments. As soon as that's completed, it's our hope the defendant will be returned to Rockland to stand trial immediately on this murder."

In the meantime, the FBI joined the search for James Sheffield.

February 2, 1981

As did most of the radio and television stations in America, we took in a feed from Punxsutawney, Pennsylvania, from some skuzzy rodent that supposedly predicts the weather.

It's free, which is why we used it. Don't tell Bob Marvin the groundhog can forecast the weather for free. It would be his excuse for firing Mark Hanock.

Punxsutawney Phil predicted six more weeks of winter. It figured.

Carl Nathe had time to kill. He always waited until every coach called in the scores of their games. Carl was conscientious to the extreme. My attitude was if they didn't call, they don't get on the air. *Fuck them.*

He had their home numbers. I told him to wait until it's very late, and then call them. If you caught them in the saddle just once, they'd remember and call you first.

Eti's uncle called me for help on a story. He wanted to know how to get publicity because the school his kids attended was about to shut. God forbid they go to public school with all the goy children.

I told him no one gave a shit. "Let's be frank. The only shot you have at news coverage would be to organize a demonstration in front of the building. You'll have about two hundred parents protesting. Then you call the news media and give them a heads up. The Associated Press could put it on their Daybook. That's all there is to it."

February 3, 1981

Steve Possell was pretty excited.

The *Journal News* did another article on him today. This one was a feature in honor of his upcoming tenth anniversary at the radio station. The last time he got publicity, the paper reported on his eviction from his trailer home around Christmas a couple of years ago.

I can't remember why. We don't make much money, but it's enough to cover the rent if you're frugal.

That wasn't the issue. The timing along with his so-called handicap was what made news. Steve had been blind from birth. He was a disk jockey. He had a great sound and the kind of personality that went over well in this rural/suburban community.

I said so-called handicap because he was low maintenance. He operated his own board. He came in early and put his commercials on Braille which he read live. He had a watch that was in Braille. I never could figure out how he cued his records. Picking albums was another story.

"The covers are all worn differently. I can tell one from another that way."

He did his own production work. He could tell the dull side of the tape from the shiny side by touch.

He engineered the board during the long afternoon newscasts. The DJs could see the news booth from the air studio. They're handed the two dozen or so carts in order. The actualities in the scripts were numbered, so we knew which ones to go to. The numbers on the carts were also on tape in Braille. Steve put them on himself.

With the other DJs, the anchors pointed at them when it was time to hit the cart. Steve fired the cart based on the news anchor's inflection. He never missed.

He also had a weekly jazz program that was second to none. He had a recent job interview at a Pittsburgh radio station which went well. Then they decided they didn't want to take a chance. Their loss!

Fifteen

Hillbilly Rain

February 5, 1981

A double murder dating from 1952 made headlines to-day. The victims were Ramapo town clerk Robert Nugent and New Jersey bank executive Charles Simpson. They were hunting in the Orange County woods about four miles west of Route 17 on a fall Saturday when they disappeared.

The legal season hadn't begun yet, so the story was they were going after squirrels.

Their bodies were found by hunters the following day. Both had been shot in the back and head at close range. A six-point buck was lying next to them. Nugent's Jeep was nearby.

Sloatsburg Police Chief Frank Dailey said the case was reopened six months ago when the sister of suspect John Youmans stepped forward.

"I believe she was sworn to secrecy by her mother, and she remained loyal to that vow. Her mother is dead. She has failing health. The murders were laying heavy on her conscience.

"So at this point in time, she wishes to bring the information to the authorities. She never contacted authorities before."

We were also dealing with a drought warning. Rockland's health commissioner proposed a three-stage plan. "Stage one would prohibit among other things non commercial car washing, serving water in restaurants unless patrons ask, and using water from fire hydrants except for fighting fires.

"If it gets bad, stage three would ban people from using more than fifty gallons of water per day in their homes."

Rockland County vicar Monsignor James Cox asked residents to pray for rain.

February 6, 1981

The way Orange County DA Edward Meyer told it, the oldest outstanding murder case in New York history was solved. "A grand jury has charged fifty-four-year-old John Youmans of Newburgh with two counts of murder in the first degree and two counts of murder in the second degree. If convicted of the crimes, Youmans could get life in prison.

"Detectives arrested Youmans as he was driving his car along Route 207 in New Windsor."

Youmans may be fifty-four, but he could pass for seventy-four. He was tall and gaunt. He wore a brown sleeveless hunting vest with faded blue jeans at his arraignment. The only thing he said was "not guilty" during the brief arraignment.

His lawyer was Seymour Greenblatt. "My client isn't guilty. He has an alibi which will be hard to prove almost thirty years later. There's bad blood in the family, and his sister has an axe to grind. That's all I can say right now."

Sixteen

Rubbing Elbows and Other Parts

Bob Marvin wanted me to produce a spot for a Dave Van Ronk concert that was to be playing in Nyack in a week. It was a charity event. Teri Thal was the public relations person and the promoter.

Dave Van Ronk was a big name in the folk scene down in the village in the early sixties. He sounded like a cross between Dr. John and Leon Russell.

Teri and I hit it off. Our politics were the same. She was very knowledgeable and articulate, so we spent a lot of time talking and a little time working.

I found out she was Bob Dylan's first manager. She put together his "Live at the Gaslight" album.

I guess some slick-haired hustler caught his ear and his purported socialist leanings went by the boards in favor of big capitalist bucks.

"I ain't gonna work on Teri's farm no more" or "Don't think twice, it's all right" reminded me of how it must have come down. I didn't ask.

We put a nice spot together. Then she invited Eti and me to the show and to the after party at the place she and her husband shared on Lake Lucille here in Rockland County.

Dan Rather replaced Walter Cronkite as anchor of the CBS Evening News. I watched Cronkite for years. He was a great one.

February 7, 1981

A senate committee began looking into claims undercover investigators from the State Liquor Authority performed sexual high-jinks at the Nyack Lounge several months ago. The Nyack Lounge was a topless and bottomless bar, which was ironically next door to the police station and village hall on Broadway.

The probers were supposedly inserting dollars into various parts of some of the workers' anatomies.

Last year, reporter Ken Voight worked on an expose of topless bars in Rockland County. His angle was to talk to the dancers to find out why they did it along with some of the pitfalls.

My guess was the money was better than kissing the bosses' asses in an office. Plus, you didn't need to know how to type.

One of the places Voight hit was the Nyack Lounge. I tagged along for "research purposes."

As we were sitting on our stools, we saw the superintendent of one of the county school districts performing oral sex on a stripper right on the bar. He was completely oblivious to everyone in the room. I guess you had to be.

Ken and I had a couple of drinks and left. No sense in doing this story. We weren't informants; we were reporters.

I took Eti to a St John's-Georgetown basketball game. She's not into sports, but she doesn't mind seeing games live. There was a priest sitting at the end of the St. John's bench. Eti asked me why he was there.

"Coach Carnesecca said he needed a good ball handler, and this guy showed up."

February 8, 1981

This pissed me off. Some miscreant stole the last rolls of toilet paper from the men's room. I wasn't holier than thou. I counted on taking them home myself. I was down to either using the newspaper or going out and buying a few rolls.

This place was a treasure trove of promotional items such as razors, pens, and pads. There was no reason to go into debt just because you want to shit, shower, and shave once in a while.

Barrie Lipscomb spent a good half hour on the line to-night with one of the village mayors. She was trying to per-suade him to get nude with her in the hot tub she had at her home.

"The human body is nothing to be ashamed of. You don't have to be uptight. It's only natural." I don't know how her husband let her get away with it, or Bob Marvin for that matter.

According to the phone tappers, she was getting plenty from the boss. I'm turning into such a yenta.

February 9, 1981

A single engine plane crash landed near the New York State Thruway in Spring Valley. It was in a parking lot.

None of the people on board were hurt.

This was notable because it was the tenth crash in nine years out of the Rockland County Airport.

Bill Haley from Bill Haley and the Comets died.

His music was life-changing for people growing up in the '50s. I couldn't get enough rock and roll after he arrived on the scene. We were among the only ones left playing his records.

He apparently had a heart attack. Haley was only 53.

We did the story and played a cut of "See You Later, Alligator" in lieu of a sound bite.

February 11, 1981

John Youmans' arraignment didn't go well. The judge ordered him held in the Orange County jail on two hundred thousand dollars bail.

He supposedly threatened his sister, Billy Kessler, after she blew the whistle on him to investigators. His lawyer said that wasn't true.

Seymour Greenblatt also said he had a witness who claimed he saw someone else near the scene of the crime. A trial date hadn't been set, so we had no idea how long You-mans would remain behind bars.

There was a big measles outbreak in Ossining, Peekskill, and Mount Kisco. It was the largest in the United States this year. That's what Westchester Health Commissioner Anita Curran told me over the phone.

I called her after she sent a news release to WRNW. We didn't get many.

"We have twenty-five cases. We've traced it to a young man from Venezuela who stayed at a local motel last month. No one is really sick. We just want people who never had the disease to get immunized."

Kenneth Gribetz: "I have a musical rapist story for you."

The Rockland DA was the best when it came to selling a story. "What do you mean?"

"This guy plays the piano or discusses music with his would be victim. Then he attacks her. These sexual assaults took place in November and December. One was at Rock-land Community College, the other at Nyack College. A grand jury indicted him today on eight counts of rape, sod-omy, and unlawful imprisonment."

Gribetz went through the gory and mostly unusable de-tails, and I had another story for the morning.

February 14, 1981

Terri Thal's house on Lake Lucille was rustic and charm-ing at the same time. I loved the view of the lake. It was Valentine's Day.

About a dozen concertgoers were at the get-together. Dave Van Ronk held court.

"You should listen to this musician who only sings one note, but he does it extremely well. His name is Dr. John."

It's funny he should say that. I didn't mention he had a similar voice quality.

I told everyone, "I had one of Dr. John's albums, 'Desitively Bonnaroo,' but I lost it. Now I can't find it in stores anywhere. That's his best album."

An older woman who was part of the opening act and whose name I forgot five minutes after I learned it said she heard Frank Sinatra recently.

"He should quit. His act is terrible. He forgot half the words, and he spends too much time berating his son Frankie Junior who's sitting next to the stage."

Peter Yarrow of Peter, Paul and Mary's name came up. Several people, including Van Ronk and Teri were very close to them at one time. Yarrow got a pardon from President Carter a couple of weeks ago.

He had been convicted over ten years ago of taking, shall we say, indecent liberties with a fourteen-year-old girl and given ninety days in the slammer.

Teri seemed to be getting progressively more nervous as the evening wore on.

I mentioned that to Eti after we left. "Well, she was married at one time to Van Ronk. Her current husband was there. I'd be nervous too."

I didn't know that. I was impressed she did.

February 15, 1981

I was getting ready to wrap up an early night when Carl Nathe called with a fucking high school hockey score. He decided to go to the game.

He also taped a seventy-second cart with details of Suffern's win over North Rockland. I had to get that on the desk for the morning sports feed.

I'd rather he covered the Rangers. More people cared about that. We'd been told more than once Rockland sports come first. It was what it was. Then Mark Hanok called with the morning weather. That went on cart as well.

There was more to this job than interviews, writing, and anchoring—including taking in feeds.

Hanok said he was working on selling real estate. "I've been at this office for six months. I have to make ends meet somehow. I didn't want to say anything to anyone at the station."

"So how have you done so far?"

"I haven't made a nickel yet."

I didn't have the heart to tell him he should take the hint.

February 16, 1981

Bob Marvin said the radio station will give a small luncheon for Steve Possell on March second to celebrate his tenth anniversary here.

Please, God, don't let it happen to me!

The affair would be held at the station. I guess Marvin worked some trade agreement with the local deli. It was free food, so it should be a full house.

I saw Carl Nathe a bit later. "Are you going to stick around another couple of years to take advantage of a luncheon in your name?"

I don't think Carl got my humor.

February 17, 1981

I never understood the way most radio stations covered court cases. They miss all the testimony. Then they come on board during closing arguments—or worse, jury deliberations.

That's how we covered the Jean Harris murder trial. Doctor Herman Tarnower became famous for coming out with the Scarsdale Diet. Harris shot him to death in the bedroom of his home in Purchase in Westchester County last March tenth.

Harris and Tarnower were lovers for fourteen years. Prosecutors say she killed him in a jealous rage.

She claimed she went to his house to commit suicide, and the gun went off as he tried to take it from her. We had two reporters at closing argument.

Rich Komonchak did the defense.

"Jean's lawyer, Joel Arnou, really laid it on thick. At some point, he had tears in his eyes. He says the diet doc was killed in a tragic accident. In other words, Harris drove there from Virginia to take her own life. She left a suicide note."

Harris was wearing sunglasses and stared straight ahead during final arguments.

Lori Siegel had the prosecution.

"They say Tarnower was killed in a jealous rage because he dropped her in favor of his office assistant."

You can never tell how deliberations will go. Fran Schneidau from WCBS-AM said Harris would be convicted. "At some point, when she was on the stand, there were jurors who were crying. She was a very sympathetic figure.

"She was a scorned woman, so they figured maybe Tarnower got what he deserved.

"That changed all of a sudden when the former girls' school headmistress looked down from her nose and called the other woman 'unintelligent,' a 'social inferior,' a 'slut,' and a 'whore.'"

Fran laughed as she said, "Guilty."

I took what Schneidau said as gospel. I felt she was hands down the best radio reporter in New York. I learned so much by just listening to her reports and figuring out how she made ordinary stories come alive. When you're a beginning reporter, your stories are usually flat. If you paid attention and emulated the best, like Fran, you could only get better.

The people at the Coachlight Dinner Theater made a last ditch effort to stay afloat. The venue which at one time brought the biggest name acts and Broadway shows to the county announced it's putting on a ladies' mud wrestling match.

The special feature would be a girl's tag team with Kitty Adams and the beautiful Susan Sexton.

Bob Marvin would have none of it. He refused to go to the mat for the venue. He wouldn't take a certified check to pay for advertising. Maybe they'd be better off.

February 18, 1981

It was a beautiful day, so I decided to take a stroll into Nyack. I ran into Bunny Crumpacker. We went to a nearby luncheonette for a sandwich.

She told me her husband, Chick, was nominated for a Grammy Award. He worked for RCA, and he put together some Broadway show music on an album.

Now I'd have to check the wires to see how he made out.

I brought up Eti and my upcoming nuptials in September. She said I was "horrible" when I mentioned our age difference. She said it jokingly. I thought she did, anyway. I bet everyone felt the same way.

Hey, what's fourteen-plus years?

February 23, 1981

Paul Giacobbe called Dave Peters with a tip about body parts being found at Nyack Hospital. Peters ran the story *New York Post* style, with shocking verbal images of legs, hands, and brains lying around.

I spoke to Dr. Zugibe about it.

"These are parts from amputees and others who were operated on. It's standard operating procedure to keep organs for two years. External parts are kept for about a month."

Fucking Giacobbe, always on the lookout for controversy. I called him.

"Hey Paul, nice story. The PR guy at Nyack Hospital wants to sue us."

"That snatch? He'd never sue. He needs you to put his shitty stories on the air."

Paul Giacobbe led a varied life, that's for sure.

Let's see. He was on the Nyack School Board where he battled against sex education. He was a law and order head of the Rockland Conservative Party. He was a former cop. He also was a former Nyack Fire Commissioner. He owned a beauty parlor where he worked as a hairdresser. He did pornographic movies. One called "Bad Habits" portrayed nuns in various weird sexual situations.

In 1974, he played a minister in an X-rated comedy film. "I took the role to increase my stage experience."

"So how do you reconcile that with your stand on sex education?"

"No one under eighteen should be watching that stuff. We don't need to put porn in schools."

He filmed "Private School Girls" at the Westgate Motel in Nyack where he usually held court.

"Right now, I'm an advance location scout for something called, 'Have You Met Mrs. Jones?' It'll be a parody of 'The Devil in Miss Jones.'"

Evan Weiner called to tell me about the Associated Press test he took the other day. He was making less at WGRC than we did in our so-called local news giant.

"I don't think I did too well."

"Why not?"

"First, they gave a vocabulary test. I hardly knew any of the words. Somehow I managed a 73. I got a 65 on the math."

"Why do you think there was math on the test, to handle our big expense accounts?"

"I don't know. Then I had to rewrite four stories. I guess I'll be at WGRC for a while. By the way, how's Eti? I haven't seen her recently."

I still hadn't told him we were getting married. It would break his heart.

Then Linda Winikow called, just to chat. She told me she watched the Eva Peron story to see how a lady got so much power. I guess she was starting to get ideas.

Here's a hint: Marry Juan Peron.

Lori Siegel asked me to listen to a couple of her air checks.

"Not bad. Keep working on it."

Lori looked at me.

"You know, Eti's really lucky. I wish I could find somebody. I thought I found Mister Right on a cruise I took recently. Everything was great. We corresponded for a while. Then he stopped. Why do you think that happened?"

"I don't know. A cruise is the worst place to meet someone you want a permanent relationship with. They're more about having a great time with someone you don't have to face after the ship docks. That goes for women as well. I'm sorry, but that's the way it is."

Carl Nathe's wife got the sports guy treatment. He dragged her to two basketball games over the weekend, plus a high school hockey game.

She had to be a saint.

February 24, 1981

Fran Schneidau was right. "Guilty."

Everyone in the courtroom waited for Jean Harris to collapse. It didn't happen. Harris was outwardly calm. One of her lawyers was crying at the verdict. Harris leaned over to console her.

Later, she said softly, "I can't sit in jail." Harris would face fifteen years to life at her sentencing next month.

She was led out of the crowded courtroom in handcuffs.

February 25, 1981

Here's something I couldn't understand. Why would someone steal money when it was absolutely guaranteed he or she'd get caught?

The super at Avon Gardens in Spring Valley had been pocketing rent receipts.

Let me guess, the books didn't balance.

Ken Gribetz told me, "This happens all the time. They take enough over a period of time that they see it as part of their salary. If they quit, it's like taking a pay cut."

"It also happens a lot with village workers who have access to parking fines. They can't bring themselves to give up the extra money."

"Look at this from the wires," I said to no one in particular. "A 707 jetliner almost crashed into the World Trade Center."

"The Argentine Airlines jet was flying at fifteen hundred feet and descending in fog Friday night when its alarm went off."

The television tower is thirteen hundred fifty feet.

"An air traffic controller ordered the plane's pilot to immediately turn right and climb."

I remember reading about a B-25 that crashed in a fog into the Empire State Building. That was in 1945.

Norwood Jackson returned our call on the Harris incarceration. Jackson is the Warden at the Westchester County Jail.

"Harris was examined by a nurse immediately upon her arrival. She also saw a psychiatrist. She'll get an orientation meeting with six other women inmates at the jail. She's in a room with a window and a wooden door. The window is covered by a wire security screen. She has to make her bed every day.

"She'll be allowed to eat in her room for the first few days. Then she'll have to eat in the dining hall. She can have as many as four visitors at any one time."

February 26, 1981

Norwood Jackson was back on the phone. "That story Harris's lawyer put out that she's on a hunger strike isn't true. Harris refused to eat prison food in her first morning at the jail. She had some snacks in the afternoon. The psychiatrist has ordered a special diet of cereal and fruit. That's not unusual."

I went with it.

I watched part of the Grammy Awards show last night, but no Bunny. I left a note on the follow sheet for someone to call Bunny's husband for a story. His real name is Chauncey, but he goes by Chick.

He didn't win. He got beat out by somebody who put together a Segovia collection from the late '20s through the '30s.

February 27, 1981

Back at WRNW, I had the usual banter with afternoon DJ Donna Donna. She had an incredible sound, which worked well at a progressive radio station. She had a great smile to her voice.

I was at my usual spot when I did my newscast. In other words, I stood and put my script on a stool that was at the corner of a simple looking board that the DJ ran. This one had slides instead of pots, or dials, that we worked at WRKL.

I wasn't sure about Donna's musical tastes. She leaned more on Punk Rock stuff, which to me was crap and on cheerful songs that I never heard of and no one ever heard again. Stuff like NRBQ, "Riding in my Car." This time she also played "Cadillac Ranch" by Bruce Springsteen. This was because the station was promoting slot car racing on Saturday. Then she led into me.

"There's a Volkswagen slot car. I'm going to see if I can get that one. Although, maybe not. They start every time but they sure don't go too fast. You want to say something, Bob?"

"At least yours starts, let's put it that way."

"I thought you were going to say yours was fast."

"You saw the smoke coming out of my car the other day, didn't you?"

"Yes," she laughed.

"Well, that wasn't from going fast."

I ran through a few stories that included federal flood relief for Port Jervis with Congressman Ben Gilman on tape, which I lifted from his handout. Hundreds of homes and businesses were affected and more than four thousand people were evacuated. I also did a measles epidemic update with Health Commissioner Anita Curran; an update on Lennon shooter Mark David Chapman, who is facing a pretrial hearing; sentencing of Marine Robert Garwood for collaborating with the enemy while a POW in Vietnam; rising gas prices with a taped quote from a state energy department spokesman; and a drug related sports story involving an all-pro linebacker from the Cowboys.

Then it was Donna's turn. "Thank you, Bob. Are you going to come down and race tomorrow for the WRNW 'Race for a Healthy Heart?'"

"You're looking at the winner."

"OK," she laughed, "I like to see a man with confidence and there's a man standing on my right who's looking challenged at the moment. Figman is shaking his head no."

"He has his tail between his legs, I can tell." We were referring to DJ Bruce Figler.

"No news nerd is going to beat me."

"I know my status around here."

This was pretty much how the WRNW newscasts went.

I took Eti to the Bottom Line on West 4th Street in New York City to catch Sippie Wallace's performance.

I think she was in her eighties. She wrote "Woman Be Wise," which said don't advertise your man because someone else will be tempted to make a play for him. Bonnie Raitt did a great cover version.

So I was at the box office taking out the tickets from my wallet when a rubber fell out. I don't know why or how I had it since I never used them.

To say it was an awkward moment would be the understatement of the year. Eti pretended she didn't see it, but maybe she did.

She never mentioned it.

March 1, 1981

The slot car race in Elmsford was pretty much a disaster because hardly anyone showed up. I thought that was pretty much to be expected since our progressive rock audience wasn't really into that stuff.

We had a very large Irish population in Rockland County. Anything that went on in Ireland was local to us. That's why we spoke to locals about the Irish prisoners who went on a hunger strike.

John Dugan of Irish Northern Aid said the strikers wanted political status, and they wanted the right to wear their own clothes instead of prison uniforms.

"They also want to receive parcels and have visitors. This had been worked out, but the Brits have reneged on the deal."

I asked whether the IRA was a terrorist group. "In Northern Ireland, young Catholics are forced into fighting back."

March 2, 1981

My car finally died. I was driving over the Tappan Zee

Bridge when I noticed thick black smoke behind me. It resembled the smoke from those convoys that crossed the Atlantic during World War II.

Bob Marvin said I could pick up a car from a rental company we have a trade deal with until I find something on my own. It was a welcome change of character from the GM.

I sold that piece of shit with more than one hundred fifty thousand miles on it to a Volkswagen place that had done some work on it in the past. I got two hundred bucks.

I got to WRKL early for Steve Possell's party. Rich Mendelson wore a suit.

"Are you going for a job interview?"

"No, I have to interview a couple of people."

One of our sales people who never showered also showed up looking spiffy in a suit. One of the DJs said he showered with the suit on to save money. Our most successful sales woman also showed up. I'm told she closed every deal with a blowjob. Hey, whatever worked.

It was only one of the sales gimmicks used here. I'll use account executive as a synonym of salesman here. I don't like big words that describe shit jobs, like sanitation engineer or mail distribution worker.

Another gimmick was where the account executive offered their mark a chance to get on the air. These store owners and their families had no talent other than making a little money. They read as if they were elated to get through thirty seconds of copy without stumbling. The words had no meaning that way.

It was what beginning broadcasters did. Then you

learned it was okay to make mistakes. The audience always understood.

Local TV stations had these losers waving their arms for emphasis. You couldn't do that on radio. It didn't matter if they sounded like shit and gained no new customers. They paid us to go from schnook to star of their small circle of friends.

Salesman Squiggy Panzarella was there talking about his Vietnam experiences. We called him Squiggy after engineer Jeff Baker recorded him at high speed to make him sound like one of the chipmunks. Some of the sound bites were used during Steve Roy's Saturday shows. Squiggy was a character on the TV show "Laverne and Shirley."

Vin the cat left a dead mouse he caught at the front lobby and made his way to the hot plates. Everyone fed him because they were afraid he'd jump on the table and befoul all the food. All we needed would have been someone playing a Bob Marvin tape. Marvin hated Vin. The cat always laid low when the GM was around.

Dave Peters sang a few songs he wrote. He wasn't bad.

The station put out a pretty good spread. I expected horse cock sandwiches and nothing else. There was hot food and a cake as well. We'll probably be running deli commercials until September.

March 3, 1981

I headed over to Budget Rent-a-Car to find out what I'd be getting. With my luck, it would be a bright orange Volkswagen they found on the side of the road.

It turned out to be a Pontiac. Nice. It had an AM/FM radio. It started; the car, that is. Life was good.

March 4, 1981

Hey, kids, bring your raincoats. Spring Valley's mayor suggested the X-rated movie theater in the heart of the village and next door to a drug den could do double duty.

The Main Street cinema will be showing matinees for children along with cartoons during Easter vacation. The theater will remain open for kids on the weekends.

Joel Rosenthal said, "It's a wonderful thing because it'll bring families, young people, and their parents back to the village. We have an ice cream store that's opening right next to the theater."

"The posters will be changed so the children aren't exposed to X-rated material."

Like they'll know what the current movie *Box Lunch* means anyway. "Hey, mom, isn't that the lady on the ivory snow box?"

"Look, *Thigh Spy*. Where's Bill Cosby?"

Seventeen

Pound Off

I might have been a great talk show host, but working WRKL's Hotline killed that. Let me start by saying the hotline was a "must listen" program and had been since the radio station got started in 1964. It ran an hour and forty-five minutes starting at 12:15 PM.

It was so controversial that a right wing group burned the radio station to the ground after a civil rights program in 1967.

Some of the hosts were loose cannons. They would get the program sued often enough that an attorney was kept on the payroll. The lawsuits would make the paper which would, in turn, increase the audience.

That format, or I should say "ruse," would bring in more advertisers. However, the show started to lose money thanks to the over the top legal expense combined with the surprise lack of sponsors.

Bob Marvin vowed to change that. No, he wasn't going to get more storeowners buying spots.

He called me into his office. "I see you as a boring person. One who won't make waves on the air. I need the hotline to be as bland as possible."

He explained the constant lawsuits. "You'll do it twice a week. Let's say Monday and Saturday. On Monday, you'll have a guest. We'll help you line them up, and you can bring in whomever you want. On Saturday, it's open mike. The radio station owner will continue to do other shows."

I'd rather do a talk show called "Pound Off." I'd go on a rant and pound the table. Callers would also be invited to pound off as well. At the end of a loser phone call, I'd shout, "Get Bent."

That was all a no-go for Marvin.

Some guests were great while others were brutal. I'd say the worst was a local human rights commissioner who was so petrified at being on the air that she shook her head yes and no to my questions not realizing this is radio and no one could see her. Her mother felt so sorry for her that she called in and carried the show for me.

We could talk in a balanced way about the big issue of the day. *Balanced* is sometimes a code word for "boring."

Deer hunting was coming to Rockland County. I'd get the head of the Palisades Interstate Park and an opponent. They'd go at it, and I'd moderate. Callers claimed they had bullets in their homes from the last hunt. "What about the children in the area?" It was the usual "not in my backyard" complaints.

Someone suggested park rangers could thin the herd

and distribute venison to hospitals and food kitchens. You could pull some tape of the comments and use them during the news. That was just one issue.

The open mikes were something else. I could bring up the deer hunt and people would call. There were regulars who prepared what they wanted to say and would read their script for way too many minutes. These were program killers. Remember, this isn't New York City or a national program; we could use all the callers we could get.

Sometimes I had to practically beg for callers. That's why the program killers remained on the air. Some were bad enough that I literally left the studio a number of times for coffee and returned in a few minutes. I knew the caller wouldn't come up to take a breath.

You could get the phones to light up with key words like "Irish hunger strike," abortion," Indian Point, Hasidim. That could get boring over time for me, but apparently not the callers.

Why Hasidim?

There were ultra orthodox Jewish sects that had been moving into the county and bringing their own laws with them. I guess that was okay, until the nature of the neighborhoods they moved into changed. In other words, a one family home became a four-family house. Two-family homes had extensions built.

Building inspectors? Many looked the other way for good reason. One was stopped by police for a traffic violation with five thousand dollars in one hundred dollar bills in his glove compartment. He said he didn't know how it got there. There are no laws against driving with money in your car.

He lost his job because they also found marijuana in

the taxpayer owned vehicle. The hotline program was on a seven-second delay to eliminate the usual *F* bomb that some callers inevitably wanted to get through.

The caller who waited several minutes just to do this would say something obscene, and they'd hear "Smile," one of the songs Charlie Chaplin wrote back in the day. You know, "Smile, though your heart is aching. Smile, even though it's breaking."

The caller would be gone in favor of the next on the line. It figures something would somehow go wrong when I was on the air.

A caller who waited a long time said nothing but "fuck, fuck, fuck, fuck, fuck . . ." which I eliminated by hitting the delay. Unfortunately, I accidently hit the same line I had cut off, so after "Smile" ended, the audience got to hear "fuck, fuck, fuck, fuck, fuck, fuck, fuck" while my hand was frozen on the caller button.

Luckily, Bob Marvin lived outside the signal range of the radio station, so no one was any the wiser.

Eighteen

What's Going On

March 5, 1981

Over at WRNW, Ron Rizzi took over for Gary Axelbank who moved on to something better. I was switched to mornings.

Axelbank hired Rizzi last fall to be a DJ.

We went to see Dire Straits at the Beacon Theater in New York City last November. Rizzi scored some free tickets.

With or without reefer, it was one of the best concerts I ever went to. They opened with "Once Upon a Time in the West," which will always be one of my all-time favorites.

The best? I'll name two. The Chambers Brothers. They opened for Delaney Bonnie and Friends. The friends included Dave Mason, Eric Clapton, and George Harrison. The Chambers Brothers were so good, that half the audience walked out during the Delaney and Bonnie performance. The second was Cannonball Adderley. I saw him and his band at the Apollo. We went to see Bill Withers and Adderley's band was the opening act. They completely wiped me out.

Rizzi went up to Willie Nile before the Dire Straits show. Nile was a folk-rock artist who just released his first album. He looked at Ron like he'd rather be talking to his proctologist. WRNW was a great radio station, but it wasn't major market. Entertainers didn't always want to be bothered unless it was someone from the big time.

Nile should have been kissing Rizzi's ass. Rizzi had some strange ideas about the business, such as radio stations existed only for the purpose of promoting products handed out by record companies. He also said he loved hearing female newscasters opposite male DJs because of the contrast. He had no clue about content.

I was on in the mornings with Bruce Figler who was probably the most knowledgeable DJ I knew. The problem with the early morning shift was I didn't know how long I'd physically last with the new hours.

Sleep was no longer an option. I couldn't cut my workload at WRKL. I know I'd have a future if I killed myself working for a real news operation.

WRNW was a job for fun and ego only. A future in the business wasn't part of that equation.

There was another problem.

Rizzi wanted Debbie Nigro and I to keep a notebook record of all the stories we did. My feeling was he should have listened to the newscasts. This would be a pain in the ass. We went from doing nothing but ripping and reading when I got here to doing a daily shitload of stories. He should have known that.

I saw on the first entry that Debbie did an interview with someone from a group called "Women Against Pornography." She was protesting a showing of *Lolita* at a local art theater. The danger of giving groups no one ever heard of air time is there may be only two or three people in the so-called organization.

I was tempted to get the other point of view from a topless dancer at the Nyack Lounge, but I didn't.

Instead, I spoke to Senator Al D'Amato on his news release about tax incentives for energy conservation. That wasn't as exciting. The senator always returned calls on his releases. His Democratic counterpart, Daniel Patrick Moynihan, never did. I guess he thought he was too good for us.

I also left my apartment in South Nyack. I couldn't sign a one year lease with my wedding coming up in September. The place was too small for the two of us.

My brother and sister-in-law let me stay at their home in Blauvelt until I made other arrangements. Their generosity was a godsend for me. I will always be grateful.

March 7, 1981

I had to calm down Suffern Mayor Joe Savarese.

First, he congratulated me on my upcoming wedding. I had no idea how he found out. Then he said, "What the fuck are you guys doing to me over there?"

"What do you mean?"

"Did you listen to your last newscast?"

"Not really, but I know what's on the desk."

"Well, listen to it. It sounds like I'm on LSD."

"Hold on."

I thought there would be something wrong with the voice quality, like a reverb or echo that would make him sound like he recorded this from Venus. It turned out there were four sentences containing four different subjects spliced together. It went something like, "We're running a great slate for the primaries: the Minneceongo creek is clean, there is no low-income housing problem in Suffern, we're close to finalizing details on a street fair."

"You're right, Joe. I'll take care of it."

The copy had Peters' initials on it.

"Hey Dave, Savarese is pissed over your story. He says it makes him sound like he's on acid or something."

"Well, we spoke for a while, and I wanted to get all the topics on, so I did a splice job."

"Yikes. It really sounds shitty. I pulled the cart."

It was similar to something Bob Marvin pulled on Steve Possell. For some reason, he wanted a reason to fire Steve, so he got one of the engineers to tape Steve's shows, then splice the on air mistakes together to make his "target" sound like a raving idiot. Steve was shaken and pissed off, but he hung on.

Dave Peters was a great guy who got along with everyone but Steve. As I mentioned before, we anchored the news from a booth that was about twenty feet from the main studio. There was a production studio in between.

We gave the DJs the carts, and we pointed to them when we wanted the actuality or sound bite to air.

With Steve, he fired the carts by the inflection in our voices. Peters' voice was really good, but his delivery was somewhat erratic. This caused Possell to misfire the carts during Peters' casts on numerous occasions.

Peters would also point at the blind man as though he was sighted when he wanted Steve to hit the cart. This resulted in more than one shouting match between the two.

Bob Marvin decided to install a buzzer that Peters would hit when he wanted the cart fired. At first, Possell would pretty much jump out of his seat when the loud buzzer went off. He also thought it was demeaning.

In ten years, he never needed a buzzer, so he didn't want this reflected on him.

March 8, 1981

I took my brother and his wife to the airport.

The money at Pan Am may have been shit, but it didn't hurt that it cost five dollars a ticket to travel anywhere in the world.

March 11, 1981

The Guardian Angels were going to Atlanta. A twentieth body had been found in a river a couple of days ago. That was twenty young black children found in nineteen months.

Curtis Sliwa and Lisa Evers were the leaders of this self-styled vigilante group based in New York.

Evers told me over the phone, "We're going down to motivate the youth of Atlanta to band together so there's a volunteer deterrent force."

Sliwa added, "It really comes down to what the community can do for itself. They need to learn how they can rid themselves of that psychology of fear. You can't do that by hiding behind locked doors."

March 12, 1981

Ron Rizzi came to me with a problem. He did an interview with Phil Collins. The problem was that he asked a question, and Collins went on for about twenty minutes without coming up for air.

This reminded me of some of the hotline callers who droned on and on and on and on. I told you my show sucked donkey dick. That was the format.

Rizzi wanted me to figure out how he could break into the taped interview every few minutes with a question, so it would sound like a back and forth.

"I'm sorry, Ron. I can't help you there. I have a day job."

March 13, 1981

The board of health began taking legal action against Nyack for not putting fluoride in the water. Representatives from Nyack, Sloatsburg, and Suffern were ordered to appear before them on March 26. The latter two villages weren't complying with the fluoride order either.

It was fifteen to life for Jean Harris. That was the minimum the judge could impose for a second-degree murder conviction.

At the sentencing, Harris said she didn't mean to murder Dr. Tarnower. "I loved him very much. I am innocent as I stand here."

A round of applause broke out in the courtroom as Mrs.

Harris sat down.

I told Ron Rizzi I was madly in love with a co-worker at WRKL. He happened to be talking about his woes in that department when it came up.

"I could never be madly in love with anyone after all I've been through with my relationships."

He was only twenty-eight, and he worked at a radio station that had some cache among the young and tender. He should have been thinking about enjoying the ride.

I began taping my newscasts at WRNW so I could put a decent air check together. The air quality was better because of the FM signal. Maybe that would help.

It was mostly being in the right place at the right time, anyway.

March 14, 1981

I turned thirty-five today. I brought Eti to meet my parents in Sunnyside, Queens.

My mother thought she resembled Loretta Young who was my grandfather's favorite actress. My father was a gourmet chef. He went out of his way to make the meal special. He started with Coquille St. Jacques. Then there was Cornish hen, which he prepared by taking the bones out without damaging the bird.

My father asked Eti if she liked licorice, and she said yes. He made a pastis out of Pernod and water. She thought strawberry Twizzlers was licorice while the rest of us thought about the black candy.

She drank the pastis like a trooper. Later, she told me she

nearly gagged.

Of course they liked Eti. Why would they not?

March 16, 1981

Belton Brims went on trial in Hackensack, New Jersey, for allegedly robbing the Woodcliff Lake Hilton at gunpoint on December 21 and a Burger King in Mahwah, New Jersey, a week earlier.

The Rockland DA said Brims will be extradited to New York once these cases are settled.

Carl Nathe said Larry Brown was coming home, sort of.

"Brown will take over as coach of the New Jersey Nets. Brown is a wanderer, that's for sure. He told his players at UCLA he finally has his dream job so maybe he'll stay put."

Brown was from Long Island. It would have been more of a homecoming if the Nets had stayed there.

The team hadn't been good since Julius Erving forced a trade to Philadelphia. He was offered to the Knicks in exchange for the Nets not having to pay an indemnity to them for switching from the ABA to the NBA. The Knicks turned the deal down. The rest is history.

Maybe Brown can change their fortunes.

March 19, 1981

A jury failed to convict Belton Brims in his robbery trial. The panel deadlocked eleven to one in favor of conviction. The judge declared a mistrial. That put the extradition to New York on hold.

March 21, 1981

A big happy birthday went out to my mom! My parents plan to be spending lots of time in France in preparation to moving there in a few years.

They're building a house in Brittany in the same community where my father was born.

Nineteen

Reagan Shot

March 30, 1981

Here's a story we'll remember for a long time: President Reagan was shot today.

We relied on wire accounts. We had plenty of reaction to localize the story, not that it needed it.

Sloatsburg Mayor Carl Wright had a day job as a social studies teacher. He was a good source to ask about presidential succession in case the worst happened.

"The law went into effect in 1947. It's the vice president followed by the speaker of the house, president pro tem of the senate. That's followed by the secretary of state and members of the cabinet in the order of their creation. The vice president would become president upon the death of the president. He would become acting president if the president becomes disabled."

Then we got the usual man on the street.

"Curtailing the sale of guns wouldn't have discouraged people like that individual from getting a gun."

"There should be a death penalty, and then this wouldn't have happened."

"We need more psychiatrists to determine who's mentally ill."

I talked to Medical Examiner Dr. Zugibe over the phone. "I didn't like the idea that he was walking into the hospital from the moment he found out he was hit."

"I guess it was symbolic," I responded. "So the country knows he's okay."

"No, he should have been brought in with the least amount of movement as possible. When the lung is collapsed, it may shift the entire chest and heart area and that kind of shift can cause death just from a collapsed lung.

"He'll be uncomfortable for a while, especially when a bullet hits a rib area. There's no reason he couldn't function quite well in a couple of days."

Press Secretary James S. Brady and two others were also shot. Brady took a bullet in the head. Some overanxious and incompetent reporter said he was dead. Someone must have said he was in grave condition, so he took it to mean he's ready to be put in the grave. Some stations ran the Brady death without checking it out further.

Twenty-five-year-old John Warnock Hinckley Junior was arrested at the scene.

March 31, 1981

The stock markets were closed today.

Gary Goldberg was our financial maven who had a highly popular Saturday morning call-in show with us that followed the Garden Hotline.

"It's done to maintain the orderliness of the markets. In 1963, when President Kennedy was shot, the market began a downward collapse. They don't want to see a recurrence of that."

The Vice President Bush-Hinckley family connection captured the attention of the newsroom. I didn't think there were too many conspiracy theorists here, but if there were . . .

"The Hinckley family and the Bushes are tight."

"They're both oil people."

"The Hinckley's have poured large amounts of money into Bush's political campaigns."

Neil Bush admitted he and his family knew John Hinckley's brother, Scott. Neil's wife, Sharon, told a Texas newspaper that Neil and Scott were to have dinner the following night.

This was how the newsroom conversation went.

"I wouldn't put it past the former CIA head to work something sinister out. He knew Nancy Reagan was still pissed off at him over last year's presidential primaries, especially the voodoo economics crack."

"Who knows?"

"Look at Alexander Haig telling everyone he's in control of the nation. He should have listened to us when we did the piece on presidential succession."

Back to the real world, John Warnock Hinckley Junior was taken to the Quantico Marine Base in Virginia. Knowing marines as well as I do, he was probably getting a good working over. He was arraigned overnight and ordered held without bond. His lawyer told the court Hinckley was an irresponsible drifter under psychiatric care.

Psychiatric tests were in the works. Nothing was said about motive.

There was a mention that Hinckley's supposed infatuation with Jody Foster was behind all this. A copy of *Catcher in the Rye* was found on a coffee table in his home.

Foster played the underage prostitute who was rescued by the Robert DeNiro in Taxi character who also tried to assassinate the presidential candidate.

Both the White House and the FBI issued news releases, saying there was no evidence of a conspiracy to assassinate the president.

"There is nothing at this point to indicate motive or conspiracy. However, it would be foolish if you etch that in stone at this point."

For his part, the president was said to be joking with doctors and nurses. He was at the George Washington University Medical Center. A hospital spokesman said the president had an excellent night.

Twenty

ABSCAM, Henna, and the Cookie Machine

ABSCAM was a name that may be remembered years from now. The scandal involved widespread political corruption. Of course, we couldn't cover it in person. That was what the AP wire was for.

New Jersey Senator Harrison Williams faced robbery and conspiracy charges. He was the seventh federal politician to face trial. Six congressmen were convicted already.

The case was based on meetings Williams had with undercover FBI agents posing as representatives of a phony Arab sheik.

Williams said he was totally innocent.

April 1, 1981

Now we knew why Governor Hugh Carey's hair color went from distinguished silver to bright, foolish-looking henna.

The old codger planned to be married on the eleventh of this month. I guessed it wasn't a coincidence that the eleventh was also his sixty-second birthday.

Evangeline Gouletas was a Chicago real estate developer. I thought her age was being kept secret. At least it was for now. Carey had been a widower since 1974. He had twelve children.

The wedding would be in New York City with the reception planned at the governor's mansion in Albany that evening.

The inmates weren't happy with conditions at the Rockland County jail.

About forty of them refused to return to their cells.

The protesters remained in a fenced yard until they got one wish: to air their grievances to a reporter from the *Journal News*.

That sucked, mainly because they were the competition. It would have been better if they wanted to talk to us. Fuck them. I'll use cleaned up tape from Sheriff Ray Lindemann:

"I'm not running a fucking Holiday Inn. If they don't like it, let them walk the straight and narrow like the rest of us."

According to the paper, the inmates wanted contact visits with family members, longer phone calls, bigger meals, and improved recreation facilities.

April 2, 1981

The people who run Indian Point agreed to install eighty-eight sirens in a ten-mile radius around the nuclear power plants. That covered about two hundred seventy thousand residents. The millions who lived outside the radius were on their own.

The price tag was one and a half million dollars. The sirens were to be installed and ready by July first.

April 3, 1981

New Jersey Senator Harrison Williams had better days, I can tell you that.

On a videotape played today at his ABSCAM trial, the Associated Press reported Williams boasted that he would use his influence to circumvent regulations on casino construction in Atlantic City on behalf of a firm his wife worked for.

On another tape played at the bribery and conspiracy trial, the lawmaker told an undercover FBI agent posing as a favor seeking Arab sheik that he would do everything in his power to help the sheik gain permanent residency in the United States.

Williams agreed to accept a one-million-dollar finder's fee for helping to arrange a seventy-million-dollar mortgage loan from the phony sheik to the casino builders.

April 6, 1981

Working the morning shift at WRNW and doing all I do at WRKL was starting to wear on me. Neither job was work, mind you, but they took up a lot of time.

The sign that it was a bit much came when I put hair spray under my arm instead of deodorant. I knew right away when my hair got stiff. At least I didn't do both armpits. I was also lucky it wasn't athlete's foot spray.

Eti said that was nothing.

"When we went to Russia, my mother brought Glade Rose air freshener with us to the hotel. When we got back to our rooms, we noticed the chambermaids smelled like the spray. They all spritzed it under their arms."

Evan Weiner called. "What's that I hear you and Eti got married?"

"No. Where did you hear that?"

"I heard something about a Tijuana quickie."

"No, but we're getting married in September. It's not official yet."

Barrie and Bob Marvin were holed up in his office for over two hours. I wondered what they're talking about. Lucky there were no springs on his desk, otherwise I'd really have a story.

April 7, 1981

Rich Mendelson made a big mistake. He bought a cookie vending machine, and he put it in the main office. He figured he'd try anything to supplement his paltry income. For a quarter, you could get a nice pack of vanilla crème cookies or cheese crackers with peanut butter in the middle or other delights.

As I mentioned before, food was fair game. We were sorry, Rich, for what was about to happen.

I gave Bunny Crumpacker a tape of original songs Dave Peters put together for her. Hopefully Chick could do something with them.

Famed jokester, activist, and former Yippee Abbie Hoffman was sentenced to three years in prison thanks to a cocaine conviction. He said he's appealing.

The thirty-six-thousand-dollar sale took place in 1973. Hoffman had been on the lam ever since. He managed to resurface several times as Barry Freed. He was even photographed with Senator Daniel Patrick Moynihan who praised him for his work on the ecology.

Hoffman's best bet would be a pardon from Governor Carey. If not, Hoffman was due to begin his sentence April 21.

April 8, 1981

Jody Foster's name resurfaced in another assassination plot against President Reagan. Edward Richardson of Drexel Hill, Pennsylvania, was ordered held on five hundred thousand dollars bail after his arraignment in federal court in Manhattan yesterday.

The secret service claimed Richardson vowed that if he failed to kill Reagan, he'd target Secretary of State Alexander Haig and North Carolina Senator Jesse Helms.

Richardson was arrested at the Port Authority Bus Terminal yesterday. He arrived there from New Haven, Connecticut.

Cleaning people at the hotel where he stayed found letters threatening to kill the president. The feds said Richardson admitted to telephoning a bomb threat yesterday to Jody Foster's dormitory at Yale University.

The secret service said Richardson shared an infatuation of the young actress with John Hinckley. Investigators said while the two lived twenty miles apart in Colorado, there was no evidence they shared a conspiracy to get the president.

There was another spill of radioactive liquid at Indian Point. This time, Westchester's health commissioner got involved.

Dr. Anita Curran stated, "Radiological specialists conducted an inspection outside the reactor building. They concluded one hundred twenty gallons of radioactive liquid had been discharged."

Con Ed said it was still trying to determine the cause of the spill. The mishap was discovered during pre-startup testing.

A group of Orthodox Jewish investors sued the village of Pomona for nearly forty-two million dollars.

They wanted to build a huge housing development on two hundred forty acres atop the pristine Cheesecote Mountain. The trustees said something like this would ruin the nature of the village. The federal suit claimed the village was discriminating against members of the Jewish faith. Ironically, four of the trustees named in the suit were Jewish.

April 9, 1981

It was arts and crafts day in the WRKL newsroom. Dave Peters fashioned a long stick out of one of the metal hangers he found in a closet. A few of us gathered around Mendelson's cookie machine. Peters put the stick in the slot where the goodies come out and stuck it straight up.

Bingo!

A pack of cookies fell out. I reinserted the stick and got the cheese crackers and peanut butter.

We'd be eating well tonight!

The village of Spring Valley was sued by a local Hasidic congregation. The group wanted to convert a private home into a synagogue. They said they had a constitutional right.

Village lawyers said the area designated for the temple was zoned only for residential dwellings.

The Hasidic group wanted a judge to decide.

April 10, 1981

Ron Rizzi mentioned female news people working well with male DJs again. I saw this as an opening.

"Hey, Ron, how about bringing in a female or two, and I'll train them before I leave here. I'm getting killed with all my hours." I knew I'd probably regret leaving at sometime down the road.

This place was really kick-ass enjoyable until Axelbank left. Rizzi wanted this to be major market. That's something that couldn't work here. Small market radio outside New York City was a pimple on an elephant's ass.

On top of that, none of the old air staff was happy. It

didn't matter to me. I didn't want this job to affect my work at WRKL.

I could only do so much.

April 12, 1981

Boxing legend Joe Louis died. He was sixty-six.

A nursing supervisor at Desert Springs Hospital said Louis had been sick for quite some time. The former heavyweight champ's heart had already stopped when he was brought to the hospital in the morning.

Here's a confession for you: I had mixed feelings about whether every male club or bar should allow women. Shouldn't there be places where a guy could let it all hang out? Some let it all hang out anyway.

When a lady came into an all-male drinking environment I frequented, you might have heard someone shout, "Watch your language, there's cunt here!"

I mentioned this because the Explorers Club in New York City voted to allow women.

The first female explorers were diver Sylvia Earle and astronaut Kathryn Sullivan. No man or woman on the planet dove deeper in the ocean than Earle. Most of the males at the club explored no more than their navels.

The women belonged—that was for sure. Ten years ago, I was an underwriter for an insurance company in New York City. There were a number of all-male bars in the area, including Whytes on Fulton Street. I understood why Whytes was forced to allow women. Business deals were made there. It was obvious corporate women would be hurt by excluding them.

I guess I'll just miss the dive bars, which have been disappearing all over the city.

Linda Winikow wasn't letting her gender hold her back. The state senator used her muscle as head of the state transportation committee to keep prices down in Rockland. This was one of the actions that made her unbeatable in November.

Bergen County, New Jersey, was closer to the city than Rockland. Still, we paid less for bus transportation to the big apple. I was at her modest house in Spring Valley today.

"I just worked out a deal that would transfer four hundred thousand dollars in state money to the Red and Tan bus company. Now the head of the county legislature is pissed off at me."

"What happened?"

"John Grant says he wasn't consulted first. He says it's an uninvited intrusion into county affairs. The bottom line is the money will ward off any fare increase for at least six months."

I'll spare you some of the salty language she used from here.

I guess you could say Winikow threw her weight around. She was heavyset. Her husband was much bigger. Still, every room in their house had large mirrors. To me, it was a sign she felt good about herself.

Rockland environmentalists came up with a new plan to reduce the deer population. Rather than let hunters or state park rangers kill the animals, they wanted veterinarians, naturalists and biologists to do it.

Marcia Beigel, ironically pronounced Beagle, was an animal rights activist. "It'll be a controlled kill. The animals will be autopsied."

Autopsied? I heard plenty of shit in my day, but this took the cake. I didn't know what autopsies would prove. I guess they wanted to find out if they died from heart attacks or brain tumors.

April 13, 1981

Poor Governor Carey. He got put through the coals over his new bride's revelations. Right now, his press people had him reaffirming his love for Evangeline Gouletas-Carey.

He was still trying to digest how many times his wife was married. Here was the release: "I am certain in my own mind that I now possess all the relevant facts about the life and marriages of my wife prior to our marriage. These matters in no way change my love and devotion for my wife. I believe her decision to be silent on her previous marriages was made in good faith to protect her child and grandchildren."

New York's forty-four-year-old first lady confirmed yesterday she had been married three times in the past. She had said she was married twice.

To make matters more complicated, her first husband turned up on the wedding day to say that, contrary to reports, he wasn't dead. She told the governor she was a widow.

A couple of weeks ago, a second marriage was revealed. That marriage turned out to be a third. And we were only joking about the governor's new hair color.

There was another turn in the John Youmans murder case. It turned out the defendant was suffering from mouth cancer.

A spokesman for Horton Memorial Hospital in Middletown said Youmans was in stable condition.

April 14, 1981

Bunny Crumpacker called at around midnight tonight.

Nyack hired a new superintendent of schools. Lori Siegel covered the story, but Bunny followed up to ask if I had everything I needed.

"Chick liked Dave Peters' music tape, and he's sending it down to Nashville. Maybe something will come of it, one never knows."

I originally suggested Nashville, so Bunny was surprised I knew in advance where it would end up.

April 15, 1981

Paul Giacobbe won his fight to maintain control of the Rockland Conservative Party.

Last September, two factions of the party got rough with each other during a reorganization meeting at the Westgate Motel in Nyack.

By rough, I mean fists were thrown, chairs flew, and cops were finally called. The meeting place was renamed "the Boom Boom Room" by the news media. A judge finally ruled in Giacobbe's favor.

I called to congratulate him and to get his reaction.

"You know, Bob, I'll back you for any office you want to

run for. If you want something local or up in Albany, assemblyman, state senator—just name it."

"No thanks, Paul. The last thing I'd like to do is get into politics."

Could you imagine a leftie like me running as a conservative? I'd never live it down.

Score one for Nyack.

The Rockland Board of Health decided to hold off imposing any fines against the village for not fluoridating its water supply. The panel voted to delay any action for sixty days. This happened after an anti-flouridationist was named to the board.

Tim Scheld called to say he'd be at the station in an hour to say hello. He wanted me to give him a critique on some tapes he made. If they were good, he'd give them to Mendelson.

Everyone in the newsroom seemed to be gaining weight. It must have been Mendelson's cookies.

April 17, 1981

Sheryl Sohn got into in even more trouble recently.

The DA said Sohn entered one of the jail offices where she was held and took two hundred ninety dollars from a file cabinet. The cash was held for fellow inmates.

She was accused of trying to mail the money to a couple of her friends so they could buy cocaine and marijuana for her. Sohn was charged with grand larceny and attempting to promote prison contraband.

Her lawyer says Sheryl maintained her innocence.

Patrick Burke said, "She claims she's being set up to take the blame for a series of jailhouse thefts."

A total of six hundred thirty dollars was missing from a file cabinet in an office that was accessible to female inmates on the third tier. No one had been charged in those disappearances.

Dozens of Rocklanders were among those who had to be evacuated from one of the twin towers. There was an electrical fire in a fan room at One World Trade Center. Several hundred workers were told to get out when smoke filled their offices.

No one was hurt.

According to the Associated Press, the alarm was sounded shortly after nine AM. The fire was confined to a room in the seventh floor service area. It was brought under control in a half hour.

Twenty-one

Danny Kaye Won't Be
Over for Passover

Entertainer Danny Kaye was honored for giving seventeen thousand dollars to UNICEF.

I only mention this because Kaye is supposedly related to Eti's father. Kaye's real name was Kaminsky. Eti's grandmother on her father's side was Minsky. Others on that side of the family go by the name, Kaye. Danny Kaye and Eti's father could be twins by the looks of them.

Eti's father was a holocaust survivor. Holocaust survivors always look for long-lost relatives. The family tried to contact Kaye about all this, but he blew them off.

Maybe he thought these were people who wanted to put the touch on him for a few dollars. Who knew?

April 18, 1981

I was elected to bring the wine for the first night of Passover. When I was growing up, the wine of choice was Manischewitz Concord Grape. This was why so few Jews are heavy drinkers.

Eti said she liked the Malaga Cream wine instead. To me, it was the difference between panther piss and goat piss.

I believed it was Saint Augustine who said in a language other than English, "When in Rome . . . " I'd be drinking Malaga Cream tonight and tomorrow night. Then it would be back to a favorite of mine, Gallo Hearty Burgundy. I knew we couldn't eat unleavened bread for the holiday.

Do cheese crackers and peanut butter count?

Twenty-two

Movie Madness

April 19, 1981

Some stories you can't make up.

First, there was more fallout from the Carey wedding fiasco. The Brooklyn Roman Catholic Archdiocese wouldn't allow the governor to be godfather for a friend's son. They said Carey's marriage wasn't sanctioned by the church because his wife was a divorcee.

The twenty-fourth body of a young black man was pulled from an Atlanta river. Fifteen-year-old Joseph Bell had been missing since March 2nd.

It's a safe bet you'd never see a movie marquee like this. In large letters:

MATINEE 2:00 PM RATED PG
EVENING 7:00 PM RATED XX.

The Spring Valley Mayor hosted dozens of kids at the matinee. He said again it was part of an overall plan to revitalize Main Street.

April 20, 1981

Ron Rizzi came in early.

"I want you to meet Claire Stevens. Can you take a couple of weeks to show her what we do here?"

Claire had a nice voice and a nicer personality.

"No problem."

Back in Rockland, a Spring Valley man who complained to police numerous times that someone was going to kill him was right after all. Theodore King had told police someone fired four bullets into his home just over two weeks ago.

The fifty-one-year-old was in the bedroom of his second-floor rooming house apartment shortly after one in the morning when he was shot seven times.

The medical examiner said it was a bullet to the heart that did him in.

Dr. Frederick Zugibe said at least two bullets entered King's body while he was lying on the ground.

Several people I spoke to in the hill neighborhood said King was a bully who beat up a number of people in the past. I got my best quote from a six-year-old.

"We all have to go sometime."

Eti and I went to see *Raging Bull* with Robert DeNiro. It was a great movie about former boxing champ Jake LaMotta.

My father hated LaMotta because he beat his favorite fighter, Middleweight Champion Marcel Cerdan. LaMotta threw Cerdan to the canvas in the first round, which injured his shoulder. He bravely took the beating LaMotta gave him.

Cerdan died in a plane crash on the way to a rematch.

LaMotta admitted he threw a previous fight in order for the mafia to set up his first bout against the champ. Years later, my father owned a diner in Lynbrook, Long Island. It had a jukebox that was serviced by LaMotta's brother. The jukeboxes were mob controlled at the time.

My father put tape on the coin slot for five of the six days we were open. He said LaMotta's brother was too much of an idiot to figure out why there was virtually no money in the machine every time he came around to collect.

Twenty-three

The Cookie Man and Other Heroes

April 21, 1981

Enough was enough.

No one wanted to damage Rich Mendelson's cookie machine. He kept boxes upon boxes of cookies piled high in his office. We'd just go in there and take those.

Abbie Hoffman apparently hadn't lost his sense of humor.

The former Yippie surrendered to begin serving his one-to three-year sentence at Sing Sing, but not before packing a book with a small hacksaw blade inside.

Hoffman was under the illusion he would serve no prison time following his conviction for selling cocaine to undercover officers. He thought he'd be working in an alternative program counseling drug addicts. Pleas to Governor Carey and hundreds of letters from friends and celebrities didn't help.

Besides the hacksaw blade bookmark, Hoffman brought with him a Chinese puzzle and a book entitled, *Fire in the Minds of Men: A History of Revolutions in 18th and 19th Century Europe.*

Hoffman said he didn't think he'd be allowed to keep the tool, but it made him feel better.

April 22, 1981

Governor Carey with his new bride at his side visited Rockland County today.

The purpose of the trip was to drum up support for a proposal that would allow the state to take over local Medicaid costs for the next seven years.

They looked like a happy couple.

April 23, 1981

No one was hurt when a small plane ran off the runway at the Ramapo Valley Airport and came to rest on nearby railroad tracks. This was a Piper single engine craft.

When the plane touched down, the pilot applied the brakes. The Piper went down an embankment and onto the tracks.

April 24, 1981

Bob Marvin was "overheard" on the office phone telling Barrie he had to get rid of some of the on-air talent because there wasn't enough money to pay us. The question, now, whose heads were on the chopping block?

You'd think at these prices, we'd all have steady work. How about goosing our crack sales staff?

We ran a shitload of public service announcements. It would have been nice if Marvin could have scrounged up a few more paying sponsors.

It didn't take Abbie Hoffman long to get back in the news.

He went on a hunger strike in sympathy with Irish prisoner Bobby Sands. Sands is getting weaker from his hunger strike. Hoffman was taken to the Downstate Mental Health Center for evaluation.

April 25, 1981

Steve Roy was getting nervous about his job.

A combination of nervousness and a finished six pack led to his latest fiasco. "I need to find out if I'm on Bob Marvin's hit list. He may be pissed because I was late a couple of times. I know he keeps new resumes in his top drawer. I'm checking it out."

Marvin's office was locked, so Steve tried to break in by going into the unlocked engineer's office, pulling out the ceiling panels and crawling next door.

That would be a tough task if you were sober. Steve wasn't.

A loud bang came from Marvin's office. Steve fell to the floor, leaving broken tiles and dust in his wake.

"Now what am I going to do?"

I told him, "You can sleep on the couch until Wally gets here. That's around six o'clock. I'll be long gone by then."

Again, Wally was our maintenance man. Luckily, there were spare tiles in the back along with a vacuum cleaner. I heard Steve and Wally set speed records cleaning the mess.

Now that was a close call.

For the second time since Election Day, President Reagan missed seeing one of his children marry.

Maureen Reagan celebrated her third marriage, this time to twenty-eight-year-old law clerk Dennis Reveil. He was twelve years younger than his new wife.

Doctors forbade the president from traveling to California. Mr. Reagan wasn't invited when his twenty-two-year-old son, Ronald, recently married twenty-nine-year-old Doria Palmieri in a New York civil ceremony.

It had to be tough touting family values when yours was as dysfunctional as everyone else's. I'm sure it bothered him that daughter Patti Davis was living and touring with Bernie Leadon of the Eagles with all their drug adventures.

He was the president. Sooner or later, they'd probably come around.

April 27, 1981

According to a *Newsweek* poll, three out of five people asked said they believed little or only some of the news. One in three said most reports were valid, and only one in twenty believed all news reports are true.

The poll came in the wake of a hoax series that won a Pulitzer. The *Washington Post* apologized for printing a fabricated story by reporter Janet Cooke.

While three in five believed it was an isolated incident, one in three said reporters often make things up.

Another small leak was discovered in a generator steam pipe at Indian Point. This happened when the plant was undergoing a series of pre-startup tests.

Twenty-four

I Can't Stop Hurting Myself

Many of the thousands of Irish people here in Rockland were glued to the situation in Northern Ireland. There was rioting in Belfast. There were clashes with police in London. This, as hunger striker Bobby Sands' condition worsened.

British police arrested twenty of his supporters.

Locally, John Finucan of the Ancient Order of Hibernians said, "The United States has a moral obligation to speak out about what's going on in Northern Ireland. President Reagan should talk to Margaret Thatcher in order to end Bobby Sands hunger strike as well as the hunger strikes of the others."

Twenty-five

Get Out of Jail Free

April 29, 1981

Rich Mendelson went behind bars today. At least he had a "get out of jail free" card with him.

Inmates at the county jail were still demonstrating for better living conditions. Rich went along with a group of county lawmakers who agreed to go in exchange for the prisoners ending their protest.

"There was food encrusted on the bars, walls, and floors. I saw peeling paint and plaster. Showers were rigged with string and rags in order to get them to work."

The inmates wanted more books in the library, contact visits, better food, cleaner conditions, and more telephone privileges. Sheriff Raymond Lindemann said he wouldn't consider a request for more mops, so trustees can do a better cleanup.

"You've got to be very careful with this one. We have some in here for high crimes. We've had plenty of mops and broom handles broken in the past couple of months. Sure they want mops to keep themselves clean. That's all well and good. But if you give a guy a mop, someone's going to be stuck in the belly with a broken handle. We're working with prisoners. We're not working with human beings."

A legislature committee approved some improvements including better lighting and ventilation. Food service was also going to be better.

Chairman John Meehan said, "I didn't realize how bad the conditions were until I saw them with my own eyes. Most of the inmates have never been given a trial. They're there because they can't make bail."

April 30, 1981

I guess the promises weren't enough. The disturbances continued.

The rough-looking suburban jail was surrounded by sheriff's deputies, Clarkstown police, and firemen. The officers said they'd use tear gas on the thirty-seven inmates who refused to return to their cells.

Others who remained inside were chanting and slamming their bars for two hours with whatever they could get hold of. Small fires were set before it all ended.

Twenty-six

Won't Get Fooled Again

The state health department had a warning about radio-active dishes. *Radioactive dishes? What's next?*

The plates in question were described as red-orange table wear. Some were collectors' items.

Commissioner David Axelrod said, "They're dangerous to eat off because of lead and radioactivity in the glaze."

"Recent testing found some of the uranium and lead based glaze emitted a small amount of radiation. This variety of cookware began to be used at around 1930 into 1970."

"The glaze flakes off when the dishes are scratched or when they come in contact with acidic items like vinegar or sauerkraut."

May 1, 1981

Senator Harrison Williams could expect to spend the next few years in prison in connection with ABSCAM. The New Jersey Democrat was convicted on one count of conspiracy and two counts of bribery, conflict of interest, and other charges.

Williams told the Associated Press on his way out of the courthouse that he was very deeply disappointed in the verdict.

He could look at the bright side. I would be a chance to brush up on his chess and tennis games at a clean, well-stocked, food-wise minimum-security facility.

The goddamn photocopy machine was on the fritz again. I had some resumes to get out, and this happened.

If I believed in God, I'd say he was steadily giving me the shaft.

I'm gone from WRNW.

I didn't get a gold watch, but I still had a shitload of LPs that they either handed to the air staff or tossed away over the months, a WRNW Frisbee, a couple of shirts and sweatshirts with the logo, plus a nice spring jacket.

May 2, 1981

The Bobby Sands hunger strike was grabbing a great deal of attention among Irish Catholics in Rockland County.

I was sure not a single Protestant ever called the radio station to weigh in. Not so with Catholics who were treated like second-class citizens in Northern Ireland.

I think Irish folk music empowered Catholics to be more militant. I don't think the civil rights and anti-war movements in this country would have been as popular if it wasn't for the musical soundtrack behind them.

John Dugan from Irish Northern Aid was one caller.

"There will be demonstrations throughout the United States. These will escalate the violence in Northern Ireland and in Great Britain. I support them 100 percent. How much do the English want from the Irish? They've been in there for eight hundred years. Don't you think it's time for them to get the hell out?"

Sands was twenty-seven. He was sentenced to fourteen years in prison in 1977 for weapons possession.

He was elected to the British Parliament last month.

The *Journal News* called Sands an IRA guerrilla. Supporters called him a volunteer. The Brits said he was a terrorist.

Score one for Billie Jean King. The tennis great showed class and courage in the face of what could have been an embarrassing shakedown by a former lover.

King admitted she had a lesbian love affair with a woman who's suing her under California's palimony law.

"I've always been honest. I'm disappointed and shocked someone has done this to people who care for her."

Billie Jean's husband and parents were at her side during the news conference.

Belton Brims was finally convicted of holding up four people at a New Jersey hotel in late December.

A trial on a second robbery could start next week. Rockland's DA hoped that would be done in time to have him tried with Sheryl Sohn later this year.

Twenty-seven

Paranoid or Just Leery?

May 3, 1981

I was looking at the pile of shit stories that were left on the desk when the phone rang.

"Is this WRKL?"

"Yes."

"My name is Sam Felder. Len Maniace of the *Journal News* said I should call you. He said you might be able to do an expose on the district attorney's office and how it targets people because of their religion. I cannot go into it right now. My phone may be bugged. Can we meet somewhere?"

I though it may be a good story. We're always on the lookout for good stuff.

"Where do you want to meet?"

"I'm in Nyack. How about at the Westgate? One o'clock tomorrow."

The Boom Boom Room was a public enough place to get together with a total stranger.

"OK, I'll be there. How will I recognize you?"

"I have dirty blond hair. I'll wear a plaid shirt."

"Got it."

Then I called Len.

"Hey, Len, do you know a Sam Felder? He called us and gave me your name."

"Oh fuck, he did call. I was trying to get rid of him. I didn't know you'd pick up. Felder is an ex-con who likes to think he knows everything that's going on in Nyack's underbelly. It's about the Zada brothers. He thinks they were all set up by Gribetz because their father is Palestinian. Personally, I think he's a paranoid schizophrenic."

"You know, Len, I covered the Shirley Smith murder in June of '79 when I first started doing news. That was the first homicide I covered in person. I also did Amer Zada's trial. He was only eighteen—a nice-looking, charismatic kid who had no shortage of friends in the courtroom. I was surprised someone like that would commit a murder. I remembered Bill Kunstler was his lawyer. I told Felder I'd meet him tomorrow at the Westgate."

"Good luck."

May 4, 1981

One of my all-time favorite musicians is gone.

Bob Marley died Monday of cancer. He was thirty-six. I can't tell you how many hours I spent listening to reggae music over the past six or seven years.

"Excuse me while I light my spliff."

Marley was the best of them.

We have no Bob Marley records at WRKL. Maybe one of the jocks will play Eric Clapton's version of his "I Shot the Sheriff."

I got to the Westgate Motor Inn at about a quarter to one.

There was a slightly pockmarked, scruffy blond man sitting at one of the tables. He had a buzz-cut prison haircut and was wearing a plaid shirt.

"You Sam?"

"Yes"

"I'm Bob. You said you had a story for us?"

"Yes, a friend of mine was railroaded by Ken Gribetz. He railroaded his two brothers as well. I can prove his innocence."

I brought my tape recorder with me.

"Do you mind going on tape? I need to get this straight. I won't use your voice on the air unless you say it's okay."

"No problem. Do you know anything about Amer Zada?"

"Yeah, I covered his trial. He was convicted of stabbing Shirley Smith to death, then sodomizing her dead body."

"That's what the DA wants you to believe. That's not what happened."

"It's what I heard. Maybe you can tell me what happened."

I had looked at the files we had on the case before I got to the Westgate to refresh my memory. We do so many stories that they sometimes run together in our minds.

I told him some of what I knew.

"It happened before sunrise. Police in Nyack heard a woman screaming near the Windjammer Restaurant not far from the Hudson River. When two officers got there, they saw a nude girl lying face down with a man on top of her."

"One of them put Zada in the patrol car while the other attended to Shirley Smith. She was dead, he was arrested. I know Smith was seventeen. Amer was eighteen."

Felder spoke, "Was anything missing, such as the murder weapon? Don't police usually pat suspects down before they're put in the patrol car? Shirley Smith was stabbed to death. Where was the knife?"

I told him, "Police recovered it in their car."

He began a long rant.

"Right. Conveniently three days later when the case was to be heard by a grand jury, the knife pops up in a squad car. What really happened was Amer's car broke down. He was checking it out when he heard screams. He went to help. He tried picking her up when cops arrived. They arrested him. They're trying to tell you they never searched their suspect, then, while handcuffed, Amer got a knife out of his jeans and put it under the seat. No fucking way.

"The cops were the only witnesses. They had to come up with a bullshit story about sodomy. Amer is a good-looking kid. He didn't have to sodomize anyone.

"They found a storeowner to testify he sold Amer a similar knife. It just so happened the storeowner was facing drug charges that were miraculously dropped.

"This was a case of a Jewish prosecutor, heavily involved in Jewish causes, getting even with a Palestinian family."

"Okay, I get all that. All of this came out at trial, and Amer was still convicted. What's different now?"

"I'll give you the name of the real killer. Let me talk to some of my contacts, and I'll get back to you."

"If you can get me the real killer along with some proof, I can do the story. What about you? Did you have any dealings with Gribetz?"

"Yeah, he fucked me real good. I admit I was selling drugs to adults only. What were my options? I had been locked up for a few misdemeanors which made it hard for me to find a job. I'm sure McDonalds was hiring, but working jobs like that would have made me significantly insignificant.

"So Gribetz entrapped me by bringing in an undercover officer to ask me for drugs. That's how that prick worked. I wouldn't have sold anything to a cop if he wasn't there. The bad deal ended with me doing a five-year bid in Sing Sing. Fuck Gribetz."

May 5, 1981

Reaction came in fast on the Bobby Sands death.

He died in the early morning hours in the Maze Prison outside Belfast. He was starting the sixty-sixth day of his hunger strike.

Congressman Ben Gilman sent an angry-sounding recording on the matter. Gilman had plenty of weight in Washington.

Unfortunately, he did what virtually every politician does. He gave the background of the case without giving an opinion.

In other words, nothing newsworthy.

Sands was the thirteenth Irish nationalist to die of a hunger strike this century. He was the first to die in Northern Ireland.

John Dugan of Irish Northern Aid weighed in, "The British government wouldn't care if every Catholic in Northern Ireland passed away. It makes no difference to them. They don't count over there.

"We'll step up demonstrations. We'll keep an eye on Frankie Hughes because Frankie Hughes is probably a few hours from death himself."

John Finucan was from Rockland's Ancient Order of Hibernians. "The death shows the brutal attitude of the British government towards the Irish people. We're also shocked at President Reagan's refusal to intercede with Margaret Thatcher on behalf of the Irish hunger strikers."

Monsignor James Cox was Roman Catholic vicar of Rockland County. He said he'll offer a memorial mass for Sands.

May 6, 1981

I went to Rich Mendelson to talk about the potential Zada documentary I might be working on.

I sat in his small office, which looked more like a cookie warehouse with boxes from floor to ceiling. Papers were randomly piled on his desk due to the lack of space.

I went through what Felder told me.

"I don't know, Rich. This would be a great story, but it's a bit shaky for me. I think his motivation is he hates Gribetz more than he loves the Zadas. I'll stay with it for a while to see how it shakes out. Do you know anything about this?"

"Yeah, I covered the two murders where Samir Zada was convicted. I remember you did the Amer case from start to finish. I think you did his wedding to his live in girlfriend after his conviction."

"No, I wasn't invited. I think someone here called Sheriff Lindemann about it and got him on tape. I know Bill Kunstler was best man. He's the family's lawyer for some reason."

"Amer's other brother, Nazir is doing fifteen years for dealing drugs. I think it was heroin. So what are you going to do when Felder gives you the name of Shirley Smith's alleged killer?"

"I'll give the information to the police. I'm not making a citizen's arrest, that's for sure. I'll have Felder on tape. I'll talk to the DA. I'll talk to Kunstler. I'll get reaction from the Zada family along with some of their friends. I'll try Shirley Smith's family. I go to the county clerk's office and check out the trial testimony. It could work out if this guy's on the level."

"Barring a confession from the alleged killer, it would be almost impossible to do a documentary in advance of an arrest. Gribetz's reputation is on the line, and it would be awful if we fucked him for no reason other than a guy who Gribetz put away wants to get even. You're right about this being shaky."

"I'll see what Kunstler says, even though I know Kunstler hates Gribetz' guts for some reason."

May 8, 1981

More than seven hundred teary-eyed worshipers showed up at St. Augustine church for the Bobby Sands memorial mass.

Monsignor Cox compared the struggle of the Catholics in Northern Ireland to the civil rights movement in the United States.

"Nonviolence is the only way to stir public support. Sands' death has brought attention to the situation there."

Linda Winikow was in a talking mood when she speculated for my ears only on her political future.

There was a story on the wire that Mario Cuomo may not run again for lieutenant governor when I asked her about it.

She said the party bosses told her if Cuomo left, his Albany post would go to either Carol Bellamy, the New York City council president—or her.

Linda said Bellamy would be the first choice, but Bellamy didn't want the job. Winikow went on tape to give me the usual political bullshit about what a great job Cuomo was doing and what a good friend he was.

My guess was, while she was telling me this, she was hoping he choked on a chicken bone or something and croaked—just in case he changed his mind and ran again on the Hugh Carey ticket.

May 9, 1981

Eti's twenty-first birthday was today. Wow, twenty-one. We had a party at her house with some of her friends from Pace University. She was young and tender. Twenty-one was young and tender.

Steve Roy really pushed the envelope this time.

He played the orgasm part of Yoko Ono's "Kiss, Kiss,

Kiss" mixed with Bob Marvin on the infamous Jack LaLanne tape saying stuff like, "Touch your toes. Get down. Harder," etc. You get the picture. I hoped no one blew the whistle this time.

May 11, 1981

I got a strange call from Sheriff Lindemann. He called me at my brother's house. How he got that number was beyond me.

"I hear you're doing a Zada-Shirley Smith story. Let me know how it turns out."

How did he know that? "Yeah, this ex con, Sam Felder says someone else did it, not Amer Zada."

"It wouldn't be beyond Gribetz to put someone away on shaky grounds, I'll tell you that."

"If there's anything you can help me with, I'd be grateful."

"I can't help you with this."

Wow!

May 12, 1981

Eti said this was the first anniversary of her arrival at WRKL. What was more important was that we started looking at wedding venues. I should say she and her parents started looking.

My contribution was I didn't want the place to look too gaudy. In other words, there should be no naked statues. I was a low-key person, and I preferred my wedding to be the same.

I had only a handful of family members. She had only a handful as well. We could probably have held the wedding in a phone booth, except her parents had tons of acquaintances they wanted to invite for business reasons.

A Con Ed whistleblower got his job back.

The labor department ordered the utility to reinstate Michael Cotter with back pay and legal expenses.

Cotter was fired January 31. The utility said Cotter was dismissed for threatening physical violence against a supervisor.

Cotter said that wasn't true. He claimed safety concerns at the nuclear power plant were minimized.

The labor department said considerable evidence existed that Cotter was fired due to his activities as a union radiation safety committeeman. He also worked as a shop steward acting on employee complaints regarding safety issues.

Cotter said once federal officials stopped visiting the plant after a January accident, conditions began to deteriorate.

In a related story, another glitch held up the restart of the plant. A utility spokesman said during testing someone noticed the water was flowing too rapidly in one of the reactor cooling pumps.

"I have to emphasize there was no rupture of the pumps. There were no leaks."

"That means we're going to have to take the plant down again, repair a damaged seal, and see if anything else has gone wrong."

Twenty-eight

A Beyond-Beautiful
Murder Victim

Sixteen-year-old Paula Bohovesky was beyond beautiful.

A witness said twenty-eight-year old Richard LaBarbara yelled "wow" when he saw her minutes before she died.

The Pearl River High School junior was beaten, raped, sodomized, and stabbed to death while on her way home from her part-time job at the public library. She stopped at the Pilgrim Market to buy a soda just before she was attacked.

This happened shortly after seven in the evening on October 28, 1980.

A friend who didn't want to be identified told me at the time, "She had that kind of presence. If you want to be dramatic, it was the kind of presence that stars have. I think that girl would have been a star had she lived. I was there the evening it happened. He mother said she was the kind of girl who if she was going to be five minutes late, she'd find a phone booth and say, 'Listen, I'm going to be late.' She didn't smoke, she didn't drink, and she didn't hang out. She was not that kind of girl."

LaBarbara and Robert McCain were accused of committing the vicious crime. Each of the former drinking buddies said he was innocent. It was the other one who did it.

Their trial began today.

Assistant DA Harvey Eilbaum outlined the case. He said the two had been drinking all afternoon at a Pearl River tavern called the High Wheeler.

"A bartender will testify they had about twenty-five mixed drinks apiece. They also smoked a couple of joints."

"They left the establishment together at around 6:30 PM. They returned an hour later. McCain was calm, but LaBarbara was disheveled."

"A witness will tell you he saw LaBarbara walking behind the victim near the vacant house where her body, nude from the waist down, was found the next morning. She was killed by the combination of a severe blow to the head and five stab wounds in the back.

"McCain confessed to police that he approached Miss Bohovesky and hit her on the head with a rock. The girl cried out as she was hit. She staggered and began to run up a driveway. McCain admits he caught his victim, then beat and raped her."

"LaBarbara spoke to police several times on October 28 about the murder and changed his story on each occasion.

"First, he told an officer he got into a fight with a man he saw assaulting a blond woman on North Main Street. He gave the officer a false home address. He said his wallet was stolen.

"Then, LaBarbara said he saw the murder and accused someone else of doing it. Finally, he said it was McCain. McCain left town for Arkansas the night of the murder."

Public Defender Peter Branti represented twenty-year-old Robert McCain. He began his opening statements.

"Young Paula Bohovesky was murdered by Richard LaBarbara, not by my client, Bobby McCain. Eyewitnesses will testify they saw Bohovesky on the night of the murder being stalked by LaBarbara.

Mitchell Schecter was LaBarbara's court appointed lawyer.

"My client never confessed to the sex slaying as did McCain. LaBarbara's name was never mentioned in McCain's confession."

Branti countered, "McCain was coerced into making a confession by police who kept drilling him for sixteen hours before his statement was taken. No witnesses will place him at the scene. They have LaBarbara blaming the murder on him and the confession. He's not the first person LaBarbara named. The others' alibis checked out. The only real so-called evidence police have on my client is a confession that was coerced out of him."

I spoke to Branti after the court session.

I asked, "Why would someone confess to something he didn't do? They can't hold him without evidence."

Branti looked closely at me. "It's not that easy. Let me spell it out for you. They get a kid and convince him they need his help to solve this case. He's on their team. He was read his Miranda rights, but they convinced him a lawyer will only mess up the investigation he's helping them with.

"Remember, my client had two dozen drinks in the course of several hours and a couple of joints. He really doesn't remember anything.

"He's given a long series of yes and no questions. The interrogators build a story from there. The cops convinced him he did it. He trusts them. He's like, 'I don't remember doing anything, but they said I did. Why would they lie? They keep wearing him down. They tell him he can go home as soon as all this is over. They write a statement, and he fills in the blanks while they're prodding him. He signs it. They arrest him. It happens all the time."

Twenty-nine

Pope Shot

May 13, 1981

Was no one immune to the terrible violence that we've seen around the globe today?

Pope John Paul II was shot. He was hit twice as he rode into St. Peter's Square. Two other people were also struck. Monsignor Cox asked people to pray for the pope's recovery.

"The pope became helpless in the matter of a few seconds, but the pope can show helpless people how to be strong."

"This wasn't an attack on Catholics. It just shows that charismatic leaders are vulnerable."

The pope was apparently okay after surgery for his bullet wounds. Italian authorities charged a suspect in the shooting. He was identified as escaped Turkish terrorist Mehmet Ali Agca. He was convicted in absentia and sentenced to death in April 1980 for murdering a Turkish newspaper editor.

We went out and got man on the street stuff on Agca. The results were pretty much surprising to me.

"He certainly didn't know what he was doing because if he did, he would never do a thing like this."

"We don't want this to develop into the persecution of any ethnic group."

"This man deserves our pity and our prayers".

"It's a disgrace."

"It's terrible people should be like this in our world today. I can't believe it. I'm very upset."

"I'm not enough of a pacifist to say there's good in everyone, but he has my prayers."

"Get him right away and finish him, right before the firing squad."

Thirty

Witnesses for the Prosecution

The Paula Bohovesky murder trial was in full swing. An Orangetown police officer testified about what he described as Richard LaBarbara's confused state.

Detective Robert Dixon told the jury that LaBarbara was questioned on several occasions over a three-day period about the murder. "First, he didn't want to get involved after coming to us in the first place. The day after the murder, he accused Tommy Wilson of the killing. The next day, he changed his mind and said it wasn't Wilson. Several witnesses told the jury they saw Bohovesky being stalked by LaBarbara.

"Three days later, on October 31, he changed his story again. That's when we told him there were too many inconsistencies. That's when LaBarbara charged McCain with the killing. Again, he told several different stories. He told me he saw McCain stalking Bohovesky. He said he followed the two of them. He saw McCain hit Paula over the head and dragged her down a driveway. Then McCain struck her in the back.

"LaBarbara said he went back to the High Wheeler bar to get a flashlight. Then he went home to change his clothes. He returned to the crime scene, found the body, and ran to police."

A twelve-year-old testified he saw the victim walking down the street with LaBarbara about ten feet behind her. LaBarbara was alone.

Barmaid Lois Weintraub testified that McCain had come in early.

"I helped arrange a ride for him to his parent's home in Monticello, Arkansas, for that evening."

"The ride was set up through the owner of a furniture warehouse across the street from the bar."

"McCain looked calm when he returned to the bar at around seven fifteen."

"LaBarbara came in a few minutes later, and he looked panic stricken. He kept saying his wallet was missing. He was sweating. His hair was all messy. He was shaking. He had a cut on the left side of his forehead."

Bouncer Joseph Ambrose told the jury LaBarbara was sloppy looking. "That's never the case with him. His pants had dirt and grass stains at the knees."

Irish hunger striker Frankie Hughes died.

Peg Matone of the Ancient Order of Hibernians said, "We won't stand idly by while British oppressors force these young men to destroy themselves as the alternative to living under British rule.

"President Reagan continues to ignore the plight of hundreds who, like Frankie Hughes and Bobby Sands have lived their whole lives under British oppression and bigotry. Why doesn't he call for human rights in Northern Ireland as he does in El Salvador and the USSR?"

We have a new freelance reporter. In other words, Bob Marvin found someone who'd work for sub-minimum wage in exchange for a foot in the door. Labor laws didn't matter in some industries. The news was one.

The tape Tim Scheld gave me to critique last month was good enough to get him a job. Rich Mendelson liked it, so he passed it on to Marvin.

I don't know if I mentioned Scheld worked here last year as an unpaid intern. He just graduated from St. Francis of Pennsylvania. He sounded good and had a good writing style already. He couldn't spell worth a shit. That wouldn't matter as long as he wasn't leaving copy for the anchors to read.

We'll send him to the usual village and school board meetings, which we cover like a glove. Today, he got to talk to Suffern Mayor Joe Savarese on a cable company postponing improvements to the village. He made it sound exciting.

In the interest of full disclosure, I was in Tim's corner because he used one of my pieces on the hostages a few months ago at his college radio station. That qualified me as a multi-state on air personality.

May 14, 1981

Paula Bohovesky's mother took the stand. Lois Bohovesky told the jury she started to worry about Paula at around 9:00 PM.

"She usually returned home from the library between seven and nine. I went to the library, but it was closed. I went to another employee's home. I was told Paula left at seven. I knew something was terribly wrong, so I went to the police."

Mrs. Bohovesky's voice cracked, "I didn't see Paula again until I had to identify her body."

After getting off the stand, Lois asked if she could be allowed to sit in the courtroom where she could hear other testimony.

"I want to learn firsthand how my daughter died. It's for my peace of mind."

The request was denied by Judge Harry Edelstein. "Witnesses are not allowed to sit in on trials. It's the law."

The mother's sobs could be heard from outside the courtroom.

Belton Brims was sentenced to a maximum fifty years in a New Jersey prison after his armed robbery conviction. He won't be eligible for parole for twenty-five years. Brims' mother passed out in the courtroom when the sentence was imposed.

This opened the way for Brims to be returned to Rockland County.

Thirty-one

Bill Kunstler "Helps Out"

May 15, 1981

I got Bill Kunstler on the phone.

"I'm Bob LeMoullec from WRKL in Rockland County. Do you remember the Zada cases? If you do, I'd like to talk to you about them."

"I remember them well. The DA up there had a vendetta against the family. That, combined with a big ego and an unquenchable thirst for power, ended with three sons being put away possibly for life. You know, I got the Stout conviction overturned about a year ago. Why do you want to know?"

"Someone named Sam Felder says Amer Zada was railroaded, and he can prove it by naming the real killer."

"I don't know Felder. You know I was best man at Amer's jailhouse wedding."

"Yes, I heard. These don't seem like cases you'd be involved with given your track record."

"Frankly, I need money like anyone else. I can't work totally pro bono while living off the largess of my wife's practice."

"I get it. Can you briefly run these cases by me? We have plenty of files here, but you might have a different perspective.

"I can, but can you come to my house in Greenwich Village? I have papers there you might be interested in."

"That would be great. It'll have to be in a few weeks, though. I'm waiting for Felder to come through for me."

"Sure. Let me know."

May 16, 1981

A man died in a pipe bomb explosion at Kennedy airport. The device was found in a men's room. A Puerto Rican nationalist group claimed responsibility.

Tim Scheld found out anchoring the Saturday morning news may be more of a trip than he realized. That was because Steve Roy ran late.

He was supposed to be there before six to turn on the transmitter and work the board for the thirty-five-minute newscast that Tim had all ready to go.

Tim called me at home. "What do I do if he doesn't show up?"

"First, turn on the transmitter. It's the one all the way to the right with four buttons. Hit the red one. It'll take a short time to fire up. Then take your carts and your copy to the air studio and sit at the board where Steve should be. The pots are labeled. Just look for the mike pot along with two pots for the carts.”

Just in the nick of time, Roy ran through the newsroom in his birthday suit, carrying his clothes. At least he had the presence of mind to hide his private parts.

“I’m late. I went on a real bender and only got home a couple of hours ago. I didn’t have time to get dressed.”

The news went off without a hitch.

May 17, 1981

Barrie just called Bob Marvin on the office phone. He waited for her at that motel on Route 202.

I guessed she got the all-clear at home.

Sheriff Ray Lindemann claimed the problems at the county jail were caused by outsiders and political meddlers. He said local judges were passing the buck to him.

“Call all the village and town justices and tell them just what the hell is going on. Every police department has cells to hold people. There are plenty of them.

“If it isn’t a violent crime, and if they’re county residents, they can be held for a couple of hours or they can be released on no bail. They don’t have to send them here to the county jail where’s it’s overcrowded.

“I can’t release anyone on their own recognizance. I can’t even let them go out on a work program and come back at night.

“Most of these legislators go to the jail, and they tell these guys they’re gonna do this and they’re gonna do that and all of a sudden, nothing happens.”

Here's where the sheriff started getting angry.

"I've been trying for fifteen years to get a decent jail, but the inmates aren't going to demand a thing as far as I'm concerned."

"They're not going to bust that jail up for nobody, I'll tell you that."

Whose idea was it to let Dan Duprey do a news voicer? He sounded much better than the rest of us, with the exception of Dave Peters and Rich Komonchak.

Jobs were scarce. Even shitty jobs were scarce. Duprey had been our morning jock for several years.

Right now, he'd be "covering" the Islanders fighting for a Stanley Cup. He was a big Islanders fan. Instead of giving him a pay raise, he got to go to the games and the post game locker room for interviews and free food.

Let's face it, this was Rockland. He was the only one in the county who gave a shit about the Islanders.

Now he was doing news voicers? Sheesh!

May 18, 1981

The pope celebrated his sixty-first birthday today. Thirty-one cardinals led prayers in a special birthday Mass for the pontiff.

He had a restful night and was moved from intensive care.

A slight earthquake was registered in Suffern.

A scientist at the Lamont Doherty lab in nearby Alpine, New Jersey, said the seismic event was picked up at Indian

Point at three twenty-two this morning.

It ran all the way to Tuxedo in Orange County.

I went to Lamont Doherty to talk to some of the seismologists. This stuff was over my head. Just show me the fucking charts.

It was extremely rare to find reporters who were as smart as their subjects.

"How come no one felt the tremor?"

"That's because it happened about four and a half miles below the earth's surface."

"It sounds good to me."

In others words, it sounded good enough for three wraps with three actualities.

The Palisades Park Commission came up with a hunting plan to satisfy everyone, but the deer that will presumably end up as sausages or stew.

Park Commissioner Nash Castro said there are twice as many deer as the system can handle.

"One hundred seventy-five permits will be handed out to hunters by the DEC. They can be used by two people—three hundred fifty hunters in all. The season will be from November 16 through December 8. That's twenty-four days. There will be no weekend hunting so hikers and campers can have the run of the place. Hunting is limited to shotguns only. One deer per person will be allowed."

Thirty-two

Courtroom Circus

Let the Belton Brims circus begin. He was in Rockland for his arraignment.

One of the most noted civil rights lawyers in the country for more than forty years was assigned to his case.

Conrad Lynn was the first black man to graduate from Syracuse University's law school. He was a national champion debater there. He was the first to go on a freedom ride. That was in 1947. He was arrested in Virginia for refusing to sit in the non-white section of the bus. People were lynched for less.

He took a case to integrate the armed forces all the way to the United States Supreme Court.

Many of his cases were legendary to this day. His autobiography, *There Is a Fountain* should be must reading in all high schools.

Brims didn't want him.

Lynn was about five feet tall with a white goatee. He looked older than his seventy-something years. He spoke in a high pitched, excited voice that made him endearing to his audience.

Brims told Judge Isaac Rubin at the arraignment, "I don't want nobody from Rockland County representing me. I want to choose my own attorney."

Judge Rubin told him, "If you can't afford an attorney, and if you don't accept a lawyer appointed by the court, you'll have to represent yourself. I'm not removing Mr. Lynn from the case."

Lynn told the judge, "I don't want to be involved in any case where the client isn't satisfied with me. I'll act as an adviser. The constitutional right of counsel also means the constitutional right of choice of counsel."

Lynn entered a not guilty plea for Brims to charges of murder, burglary, robbery, and grand larceny in connection with the Sohn killings.

Outside, Lynn said, "I don't want to do this. This is a dreadful case because it's about a daughter who hires two men to kill her parents. People tend to confuse the lawyer with the defendant as if the lawyer was in cahoots with him when the crime was committed. I've had some tough cases where people asked, 'How could you defend that person?'"

"A defendant is entitled to counsel, but this is a bad case."

The United States Mission to the United Nations was evacuated when a pipe bomb was found there Sunday. The device was similar to one that was removed the same day from the Pan American terminal at Kennedy Airport.

Two bombs were found Saturday. One exploded, killing a man. A Puerto Rican nationalist group claimed responsibility.

May 19, 1981

The Robert McCain confession took center stage at the Bohovesky trial. Inspector Peter Modafferi told the jury he called McCain at his Arkansas home and asked if he'd come to New York to answer questions.

"McCain said he hadn't done anything, so he'd be willing to go. Later he said he'll go to straighten things out since no one has accused him.

"I said a young girl is dead. You can't tell me you can't remember things you should remember. I was taken by surprise when he said, 'Maybe I killed her. I can't remember.' He was read his rights. Back in New York, we questioned him for about an hour and a half at Orangetown police headquarters. I wasn't there until the end.

"He gave us written and oral statements to the effect he was drinking heavily during the afternoon of October 28. He said he was sick and decided to take a walk on Central Avenue. That's when he noticed Miss Bohovesky. He picked up a rock and threw it at her. He didn't know why he did it. He said the blonde girl was startled and started to run. He started hitting her. He knocked her down, pulled down her pants, and raped her. McCain was crying when he told the story. He said he was sorry and must be sick. He said, 'You must hate me.'

"McCain became sick again after the statements were

taken. He was hyperventilating and lying on the floor. A doctor came in and gave him oxygen.

"McCain said it wasn't his fault. He had a violent childhood. He suffered from seizures and would get violent but couldn't remember what he did afterwards."

Detective Raymond Lundy was the officer who got the confession. "He kept telling us he couldn't remember anything. I decided the good guy approach wasn't working so I raised my voice. I told him to knock it off. We're not here to play games. This is serious. McCain began crying and put his head on my shoulder. He kept saying, 'I did hit her, I did hit her.'"

Next, a friend of Richard LaBarbara provided damaging evidence against the McCain codefendant.

Richard Spielman was shown a folding knife that was entered into evidence. Spielman testified he threw LaBarbara's knife into a lake in Tappan after wiping off the prints.

"I did it a few days after the murder. There was no blood on the knife, but Richard told me it would be better to get rid of it. I visited him in jail and asked him if he did it. He said he was so drunk, he didn't remember. He said McCain was trying to pin it on him."

Conrad Lynn tried again to withdraw from the Brims case.

"This is what I told the judge. Brims won't confide in me. All during the trial, he'll feel he's being railroaded. Especially in this case where he thinks I have too friendly a basis with Mr. Gribetz. He thinks any Rockland County lawyer would be too friendly with the district attorney. Let me be frank here. No lawyer would welcome that case because it is really such a bad case. Once the facts are out it's going to be very bad. The unfortunate thing is that the people begin to ascribe the savagery of the defendant to his lawyer."

Mr. Lynn laughed in his high-pitched squeal as he went on.

"People have called me up on other cases and asked me, 'Why did you defend that man?' Don't you think a man who's committed a crime like that should meet his punishment?' I've been called on the phone by friends many times on other cases with the same message."

Thirty-three

Newsdesk Follies

A fire at a Hasidic boy's school in Hillcrest again had Rockland officials concerned.

They had been trying for months to shut the yeshiva in the former community hospital building due to numerous code violations. Some of the violations included blocked hallways, improper fire doors, and garbage jamming some of the rooms along with leftover medical supplies.

No one was in the building when the early morning fire started. The inspectors got a court order to close the school until the violations were straightened out.

May 20, 1981

I called Sam Felder to check on the status of his sources. "Just remember the name Gensel. Samir was convicted of killing Jerry Stout, and a few months later, Christian Gunther. Gensel admits he was at both. Ask yourself why he's walking free today. I can't say anything more over the phone. I'll get in touch with you."

"Why not over the phone? You don't think there's anything to be paranoid about at this point, do you?"

"I'm not paranoid. I'm leery."

May 21, 1981

There was no talking with Dan Duprey today.

His Islanders won the Stanley Cup for the second straight year. They beat the Minnesota North Stars four games to one with a five-to-one victory at the Nassau Coliseum.

A minor school bus crash caught our attention.

These accidents were a high priority ever since the Congers bus crash of 1972. Five kids died and dozens were hurt when the driver raced a train to a crossing and lost.

In this case, five of the children were admitted to Nyack hospital while several others were treated and released. The kids were all students at St. Anthony's Parochial school in Nanuet.

May 22, 1981

The Rockland Board of Health may rescind the fluoridation mandate we've been talking about since the beginning of the year. When first voted on, it was four in favor and three opposed. With new members in and old ones out, the majority turned.

The state health department in Albany would have the final say.

It was curtains for the Coachlight Dinner Theater. The owners said ticketholders could get credit toward other shows. How was that going to happen with the place boarded up?

You might try to get a refund. Just wait in line.

May 23, 1981

"How about Bear Mountain?"

Eti was thinking about wedding places again. I thought it would be a good idea because of our history there. It was a rustic yet romantic setting. There was a big stone fireplace inside the main room that was made out of logs. The wedding was planned for what was an early fall in the lower Catskills, so there might be some color on the trees. The symbolism would be good.

As Camus wrote, "Autumn is a second spring where the leaves turn to flowers."

On the other hand, the food was probably shit city. I brought up another consideration. "It's a bit out of the way. How are your parents' friends from Long Island and New Jersey going to get there?"

"Yeah, that's out. Too bad."

We visited one place on the Hudson River near north Yonkers. It had a great view, but the venue itself had an American Legion Hall look to it. That was out as well.

May 26, 1981

Sam Felder called to find out if anything was going on with Zada. Was this guy giving me head, or what?

"I'm waiting for you. No one came in to tearfully confess their crime to me."

"I didn't think so."

He thought I was serious. How did I get into this, anyway?

"Give me a quick briefing on the Jerry Stout and Christian Gunther murders. They happened in 1973 before Gribetz was DA."

"He was the top assistant. You have to understand; Gribetz is well-known for getting involved with pro-Israel causes. He'll be in Manhattan in a couple of days to head up a parade in favor of Jews in the Soviet Union. It's a feather in his cap to put away three Palestinian brothers."

I could see the skin-headed direction this was taking. No fucking way.

"OK, so what happened in the murder cases?"

"What I know about the Gunther case is he was a plumber from Congers. Fred Gensel's father worked for him. Gensel wanted to rob him, so he got Samir Zada and a couple of other guys to go to Gunther's house. They stuck him in the trunk of his car and drove him to a wooded area. Gunther got out and started running. The word on the street was Gensel shot him because he didn't want a witness who knew him to remain alive. The DA blamed Zada and got Gensel and a few others to testify against him in exchange for no time in prison.

"In the other case, the guys were friends with Stout. He was a dance instructor. They knew him from the Comeback bar in Piermont across the street from the Diplomat Apartments."

"I lived at the Diplomat when I first came to Rockland," I volunteered. "I never went to the bar, though."

"It was a gay bar. Zada and Gensel were straight, but they went there on occasion. Zada was no saint. Stout had this big ring, and the guys got the idea they should steal it. They went to Stout's apartment where he lived with his mother."

It was the Regency Apartments in Spring Valley where coincidentally Gribetz also lived. Stout ended up dead. Zada caught the rap, and Gensel testified against him and got away scot-free.

"A third brother, Nazir, was set up as well. He's doing a long bid for supposedly selling heroin."

I didn't know what I had—probably nothing. I decided to talk to Bill Kunstler before I went forward.

May 27, 1981

There were stories you were guaranteed to write every year.

In the summer, it was drowning. It happened yesterday in Haverstraw.

Three young men were swimming in the Hudson River when one began having trouble staying afloat. Police were called when a bystander ran to the post office and yelled for help. Rescue boats arrived. Two swimmers managed to get to shore.

Reynoldo Matos didn't.

Scuba teams continued to look for his body.

Getting back to the Bohovesky trial, two experts testified they couldn't say for sure whether dried blood found on the clothing of Robert McCain and Richard LaBarbara belonged to Paula Bohovesky.

A small stain with the victim's blood type was found on a leather belt that belonged to McCain. McCain was wearing that belt on the day of the killing.

It contained Bohovesky's rare A-B blood type.

A similar stain was found on LaBarbara's underpants. There were no signs of blood on LaBarbara's jeans, which were found on the side of a road in Rockland County. His knife was recovered from a lake.

Indian Point was back in business. *Almost.* It went up to 50 percent power and could be at full capacity in two weeks.

It took four tries to get it going. For some reason it kept shutting down.

A Con Ed spokesman says this wasn't unusual.

May 28, 1981

Dr. Frederick Zugibe testified head and throat injuries suffered by Paula Bohovesky left her unconscious and dying.

The Rockland medical examiner was the final prosecution witness. "She immediately went into shock. Her body was found on its stomach."

This was different from McCain's confession, which had her lying on her back.

"She was unconscious when she was stabbed five times in the back. I found no evidence the victim was raped. The girl suffered injuries consistent with sodomy, but I can't say with certainty she was sodomized. There was no struggle."

This was also different from McCain's confession. He admitted raping the victim but said nothing about stabbing and sodomizing her.

"Paula died within ninety minutes. One of the knife wounds collapsed the victim's lung. The knife that was used was consistent with the folding knife entered as evidence."

Indian Point was off-line again. Con Ed said it was to adjust a cooling oil system in a non-nuclear part of the plant.

They always threw that in when they could.

Engineers planned to test the system this week while increasing capacity. The Nuclear Regulatory Commission ordered Con Ed to pay two hundred ten thousand dollars in fines for flooding earlier this year.

Of course, this would be passed along to the ratepayers.

May 29, 1981

I was surprised that after the big deal public defender Peter Branti made about his client's confession, he never mentioned it in McCain's defense. I was not surprised McCain didn't take the stand. He didn't have to.

The public defender said later he kept his client off the stand because the prosecution failed to make a case against him. Branti called James McCain, Robert's father as his only witness.

His main purpose was to explain how Paula Bohovesky's AB blood type got on Robert McCain's belt.

The very rare blood type was the only evidence other than the confession linking the defendant to the crime.

James McCain testified about handling the belt. "The belt was unusual. Not a man's belt. It had butterflies, mushrooms, and flowers.

"I picked it up to take a look at it. I had cuts on my hand from my job making Styrofoam. Some of it might have gotten on the belt."

Branti asked, "What's your blood type?"

"AB."

May 30, 1981

A helicopter bound for the Ramapo Valley airport in Rockland crashed in Westchester. The chopper narrowly missed several homes before striking a power line shortly after eleven Friday night. The fiery crash killed the pilot and his passenger.

There was one witness.

"I heard the plane circling low around my house when it suddenly hit the wires. I found an engine on my front porch."

Thirty-four

Burglary Can Be Hazardous to Your Health

May 31, 1981

A Ramapo police officer killed an unarmed burglary suspect in Monsey today. Investigators said Officer David Lamond shot Neil Bernstein after the suspect jumped from a second-floor window and tried to get away.

Bernstein was pronounced dead from a gunshot wound to the head.

DA Kenneth Gribetz held a news conference at Ramapo Police Headquarters within a couple of hours after the shooting.

"We're conducting an investigation concerning all the facts and circumstances surrounding this incident. All evidence that has been recovered by the Town of Ramapo Police

Department as well as investigators from my office will be presented shortly before a grand jury. It'll make the ultimate determination as to whether any charges will be brought against Officer Lamond."

Grand juries almost never brought indictments against police officers for good reason. It was up to prosecutors to present a case. They bring in evidence that makes the bad guy look really bad. There would be virtually no evidence brought against the cop. It was called burying the case in the grand jury. It gave the politicians a chance to scream for justice while knowing there would be no chance for an indictment.

I didn't know Lamond. It would be completely unfair to say at this point whether the officer had a dislike for men wearing yarmulkes. I doubted anyone would ask.

According to Gribetz, "Witnesses had seen Bernstein kick in a window and enter a house on Forshay Road, two houses down the block from where he lived with his parents. A neighbor called police at about 4:00 PM, and Officer David Lamond responded. He entered the home while the burglary was still going on. Bernstein climbed out the bedroom window in the rear of the house. He went six feet before he was shot. Bernstein did not have any stolen property in his possession. A witness tells us he was picking up his yarmulke when the shooting occurred. He may have been turning toward the officer. We believe Lamond mistook it for a gun."

"Bernstein had been free on twenty-five hundred dollars bond stemming from a charge of possession of stolen property. That incident occurred April 23."

Police Chief Joseph Miele said Lamond was placed on administrative leave. "Burglarizing homes can be hazardous to your health."

Gribetz glared at him.

June 1, 1981

Dr. Zugibe called us after he completed his autopsy on Bernstein.

"The autopsy findings revealed a gunshot wound to the back of the head. It's consistent with being shot in the back of the head while the person was leaving the scene. We recovered the bullet. It penetrated the skull and passed into the brain. We submitted it to the police lab."

Thirty-five

The Beat Goes On

Let me remind you again we wrote dozens of stories that wouldn't ever be an asterisk in Rockland history. It was mainly to build a local audience while filling an incredible number of news minutes we had to put out every day. Here was an example:

Rockland legislator Sandy Rubinstein sent us a news release saying he didn't want to see tolls on the Palisades Interstate Parkway. There might have been rumblings about it. So we called him to get a couple of sound bites.

"It's a two-state roadway. We can't control what New Jersey does. We can go on record saying New Yorkers don't want tolls on that road."

In other words, he had nothing. Whether Rubinstein liked it or not, he had absolutely no say in the matter.

We got the Parkway commissioner who admitted the

matter was under review.

That relegated Rubinstein's story to "reaction."

June 2, 1981

Rape charges against Robert McCain and Richard La-Barbera were dropped. Judge Harry Edelstein said the prosecution failed to prove the victim was raped during the attack that claimed her life.

"The failure to corroborate the rape charge based on the confession leads me to dismiss it."

The judge declined to drop the murder charges against either of the defendants. McCain's case was rested Friday.

Mitchell Schecter's defense focused mainly on police isolating LaBarbera from friends and family during questioning. LaBarbera didn't take the stand.

June 3, 1981

The defense lawyers for McCain and LaBarbera went after each other during final summations.

Peter Branti said his client never ran and never hid.

"The four confessions were spoon-fed by investigators. My client is just a boy who was terrified.

"He was taken from Arkansas to New York without luggage or money. He even offered to take a lie detector test, which police never gave him.

"Only LaBarbera fingered him. That only happened when police told him the other man he fingered had an alibi. No one else saw McCain at the crime scene. Not one person."

Mitchell Schecter told the jury the murder of Bohovesky was horrible.

"It would be worse if you convict an innocent man. Only one man confessed to the murder and that was McCain, not LaBarbera. My client made up some of his stories because he wanted police to find the body. He didn't even think of hiding his knife until a friend suggested it because police were harassing him."

In his closing argument, prosecutor Harvey Eilbaum told the jury McCain confessed to the crime.

"He told investigators he hit her on the head and raped her. LaBarbera then turned her over and sodomized her, then stabbed her five times before running. McCain was calm in the bar because he knew he was leaving that night for Arkansas.

"LaBarbera changed his story four times. He said he didn't do anything, yet he had a friend get rid of his knife."

A yeshiva in Hillcrest that was recently ordered shut by a judge because of numerous fire violations remained open.

Ramapo asked for a contempt of court citation against the group running the school. How parents could allow their kids to go to class under dangerous conditions like these without complaint was beyond me.

June 4, 1981

Did former Yippee Abbie Hoffman lead a charmed life, or what?

He got a part-time "get out of jail free" pass after serving a little more than a month at Sing Sing. He was placed at a minimum security prison on West 110th Street in Manhattan on a work release program. He'd be allowed to leave the facility for his job, then to return at night.

Hoffman was also eligible for weekend furloughs.

June 5, 1981

We hit a couple more places in our search for a wedding hall.

The first was in Rockleigh, New Jersey. It looked great. It would be convenient for guests to get there. Then the manager came up with his piece de resistance. He opened a curtain in the main ballroom, and hidden behind it was a waterfall. I'm outta here.

Next was the Tarrytown Hilton. That was the most convenient for travelers since it was right off the thruway. It had a stone fireplace that reminded us of Bear Mountain. The manager let us try the food, which was exceptional. There was room for a combination indoor/outdoor cocktail hour. We could also have an outdoor wedding if the weather was nice with an indoor reception.

We found our place.

June 6, 1981

Robert McCain and Richard LaBarbera were both found guilty of two counts of second-degree murder. The two defendants sat motionless when the jury's verdict was read. They were acquitted of intentional murder and sodomy.

We had our news team getting reaction.

Lois Bohovesky, the mother of the victim, spoke first.

She was shaking, and her voice was cracking.

"We had support from everybody. If we hadn't, I don't think we could have come through this with one shred of sanity. To lose a daughter, to lose a child, my God, is something you just can't comprehend. No matter what happens, no matter what they do, Paula's not coming back. She's not going to be my girl in twenty-five years. She won't be up for parole, and she didn't even do anything."

Paula's father, Basil, was shaken and soft-spoken.

"I was disappointed that the intentional murder charge wasn't decided as guilty. I feel there was intent to commit murder. I feel five stab wounds is very clearly intent. I think three stab wounds are clearly intent."

Peter Branti said he'll appeal.

"I think there are grounds for reversal here in light of the fact that the fourth count of the indictment, which is the alleged rape, was dismissed at the end of the people's case. The judge failed to notify the jury of that until after I rested my case. It was based on that decision that I couldn't put my client on the witness stand."

Mitchell Schecter also talked about an appeal.

"There are various areas which we'll explore vigorously. I believe severance should have been granted. The defenses of the two men were antagonistic and never should have been heard together. That's a real appellate issue."

Prosecutor Harvey Eilbaum said he had a strong case. "We had confessions McCain made implicating himself. It's true he never implicated LaBarbera, but he had implicated himself. You can see the jury didn't believe he was force fed these statements."

The verdict didn't come until the evening. Earlier, I got a chance to cover a Governor Carey ribbon cutting in Congers, not far from the courthouse.

It was my first time tasting sake. A Japanese firm planned to open a machine tooling company, which would bring sixty-five jobs to the county.

The sake was part of a toast. The other part was the governor touting New York State as an economic destination.

"It's one more sign that in looking everywhere, the prudent businessman decides to settle in New York. We can match and compete with any state in the union. We can offer skilled labor as well as tax advantages."

With our huge news load, we could never, ever let the governor go without news desk filler. I was reluctant to ask him how he found married life.

I know I probably should have. I asked about Medicaid and transit fares.

"The subway fare will go to seventy-five cents in July and be frozen there for two years. Commutation fares in suburban counties will also be maintained for at least two years."

That was news to us.

June 8, 1981

Israel caught serious heat from the Reagan administration for bombing an Iraqi nuclear reactor in Baghdad yesterday.

The state department immediately issued a statement of condemnation. Israel said the plant was not for nuclear power, but for nuclear weapons, adding the air strike was an act of self-defense.

Reagan aligned himself with the Arab governments. They called it an act of terrorism.

Even Iran, which had been at war with Iraq for the past nine months, condemned the attack. Local reaction was overwhelmingly pro-Israel. County Legislator Sandy Rubinstein said there was no other way.

"The Israeli government always does what it has to do to survive. That's what keeps it strong."

Reverend Richard Deats of the peace group Fellowship of Reconciliation had a different view.

"The bombing is extremely provocative. Such a preemptive strike opens the door to greater violence in the area."

June 9, 1981

Dave Saviet asked me if a friend of his could come in to make an air check that he'd produce for her.

He worked here at one time. Dave was far from being a homophobe, but he would always talk with a lisp when Bob Marvin was around.

That's because he loved to watch the veins in Marvin's neck bulge. I think Marvin eventually fired him for that reason. Dave got a job at the CBS Radio Network doing brilliant production work that was aired nationwide.

I had no problem with friends using the equipment. I didn't think Dave told her to keep it low and keep it slow. Yvonne Mobley sounded great. She'll do well—maybe better than us.

June 10, 1981

I finally hooked up with Bill Kunstler on the Zada case.

It was more about curiosity at this point. Somehow, I'm doing the bidding of a paranoid skinhead. I hate being jerked off. Remember, I did this on my time for free.

"My place is on Gay Street in the village. The address is 13 Gay Street between Christopher Street and Waverly Place. It's only one block long."

I remembered seeing a man/boy love demonstration near there a while back. It was a bunch of NAMBLA members holding signs that read, "Young boys need love too!"

Tim Scheld tagged along so I wouldn't be stuck going all the way down there alone. The place, 13 Gay Street, was a triplex. Kunstler lived on the top two floors. His office was on the first floor. It was a neat space with brick walls and a working fireplace. He probably bought the old place for peanuts.

"You know, Harriet Tubman lived here before the Civil War. This house was a stop on the underground railroad in the late 1850s."

I could hear the pride in Kunstler's voice. He must have felt the thread that ran from the protesters back then to the present time where he was a major player. In this case, he dealt with a family of convicts who happen to be Palestinian. I wouldn't say he was a self-hating Jew, but I didn't see him getting involved with Jewish causes either.

"This is not a civil rights case. I don't care about their ethnic background. I don't like to see defendants become victims of prosecutorial misconduct.

"Here are some of the files you can go through. I think I told you I helped win a reversal of the verdict in the Stout case."

"What was the big issue?"

"It's in the file. Basically, there was a gaudy ring that Zada sold to a jeweler in Nyack. The judge erred when he implied to the jury that if Zada had the ring, he must have stolen it. Zada insisted he got it from someone who found it."

"What about the misconduct?"

"Gribetz leaned on people who faced criminal charges themselves to testify against the Zadas. He had one witness who was at the scene of two murders wired to talk to other witnesses. To me, this isn't about Palestinians. The three brothers' father is from Turkey. This is about a prosecutor who'll cheat to win at all costs."

Tim and I spent about an hour going through Kunstler's files. There was nothing there I didn't know before. I thanked him for his time and hospitality, and we left.

June 11, 1981

Linda Winikow pushed through a resolution in the state senate that told the Palisades Park Commission it was against turning the PIP into a toll road. This didn't mean the commission couldn't do what it wanted.

Resolutions are just the product of lawmakers whacking off, then sending the result in a mailing to prospective voters.

Winikow said Rocklanders entering New Jersey would be the first to be hit. "This was built with federal money. It was never designed to be a toll road. We in Albany are telling the five members on the commission who are appointed by us that in no way do we want them supporting any studies, any thinking, any tolls."

A random search of the Rockland County jail netted a treasure trove of contraband.

District Attorney Kenneth Gribetz said one of the prisoners was charged with criminal possession of a weapon and promoting prison contraband.

"He had a metal spike fashioned out of a pen and a portion of a broom. It was found in his cell. He also had a forty-foot escape rope made from bed sheets braided together. Dozens of items that could be used to make weapons were found in a common area of the jail. Guards also found thirty gallons of home brew made up of fruit juice, yeast, and Aqua Velva."

In part, local news was done this way: we reported something may happen. When it did, we reported that. Then we followed it up with reaction. The fluoride story was a prime example. We'd been beating this story to death since the beginning of the year.

Well, the Rockland Board of Health overturned the fluoride law. Pro-fluoride people said the water company and some village boards just waited it out until the dynamic of the board was changed.

Now it would be up to Albany. Stay tuned.

June 13, 1981

Major League baseball players went on strike. Both sides were battling over free-agent compensation.

The team owners wanted to be given another player if

they lost a free agent. The players said this would restrict their movement between teams. We got local reaction.

"I just took part in a teachers' strike, so I tend to believe management is unfair."

"I think most of them make too much money now."

"I don't like the free-agent system. The Yankees are a good example. Steinbrenner bought that team."

"I don't think they're entitled to what they're asking for."

"I don't follow baseball much anymore."

June 14, 1981

There was a pretty bad fire overnight at a school in Monsey run by a Hasidic sect.

Fire Coordinator Don Hastings said luckily the department was only blocks away.

"There were no sprinklers and no smoke detectors. When firefighters arrived, there were flames coming through the roof. There were excessive amounts of flammable materials in the school. There were several rooms that were filled with household furnishings such as stuffed chairs, sofas, beds, dressers, and televisions. The rooms were literally filled almost up to the ceilings. The school was doubling as a warehouse for storage."

Summonses were issued for storage of combustibles.

Thirty-six

Teach Me Tonight

June 15, 1981

Rich Mendelson told me we have a new freelance reporter on board.

"Bob Marvin told me Barrie Lipscomb wants to learn that aspect of the business. You can send her to Haverstraw. There's an exciting meeting going on there tonight."

Low-income senior housing would be the big story. That would bring out a crowd of pros and cons. Barrie came in all excited with a tape recorder and mike she just bought along with a reporter pad and some pens. I gave her a WRKL mike flag to put on the microphone. That way she'd look like a pro.

"You have batteries, right?"

"Yes, I just bought them," she said enthusiastically

"OK, here's a brief primer. Get there early. Ask a few

people what's going on. The key to good reporting is knowing the issues. Don't be afraid to ask questions. You don't need tape up front, but it might be a good idea to get some. You never know. Your recorder has a tape counter. You can mark down the numbers where you have good sound bites. That way you won't have to go through hours of tape when you get back here.

"People are probably going to go to a podium to give mini speeches. That would be your best bet. Don't be reluctant to put your mike at least six inches from their mouths. If you put it farther than that, the sound will be unusable. Get both sides. Avoid politicians. They'll give you a bunch of self-serving shit, and they're usually boring anyway.

"There's another thing. Don't give your opinion. We actually had a couple of reporters who went to the podium to give a speech. There's no way we should be doing that."

I went through the tape with Barrie after she returned. I let her write her story. She had a lead sentence that was about forty words long.

"You can't stuff ten pounds of shit in a two-pound bag. Keep all your sentences short. You should have one idea per sentence. We don't need people's ages unless there's something remarkable about it."

At this point, she was standing against me. She put on some of her patented charm. Then she put a motel key on the desk in front of me.

"This is where I'll be staying tonight."

"Sorry, Barrie. I'm engaged."

"Well, you're not married yet."

I had no business judging anyone. I was a male 'ho' not very long ago. My credo was if she consented, she was fair game. I was lucky enough to have been with some of the most intelligent and beautiful women on the planet.

Now I had the best. Why fuck it up? I had a couple of virtues. One was loyalty.

Also, if you told me something in confidence, it stayed there. We all have our pasts. I could write a book on all the private confessions I heard. I'd take a confidence with me to the grave.

"Don't take it personally, Barrie, but I'm not interested."

Thirty-seven

Summertime Blues

June 16, 1981

I was getting tired of this story.

A couple of malfunctions closed Indian Point again. *Guess what?*

A company spokesman said neither of the problems took place in the nuclear portion of the plant.

"There was no leak of radiation, and no danger to the public or utility workers. It shut itself off at twelve thirty the previous afternoon when a valve that carries steam to a turbine closed. That happened just twelve hours after the plant was put back into operation following a shutdown Monday. Right now, the plant is operating normally."

June 18, 1981

You could chalk one up for Linda Winikow. The idea of tolls on the Palisades Interstate Parkway was shelved.

The commission wanted to put the issue on hold for a couple of months.

Winikow demanded a decision right away. Fortunately, it went her way.

My mother-in-law to be got her name in the newspaper today. No, she wasn't arrested. She made a list of locals who got their bachelor's degrees from Empire State College. The graduation was held at SUNY Purchase in Westchester.

Eti put together a thirty-foot poster with words to the effect, "We are proud of our mom."

I'm a low-key guy, so I had to slink in my seat while sitting in the back row holding my part of the sign. This should be a warning to me.

June 19, 1981

Three times a year, the radio station partnered with the Nanuet National Bank to hand out Athletes of the Season awards.

It was a big day for Carl Nathe. Not only did he get his picture in the *Journal News*, he got a free meal at the Hungry Lion. That was no small deal at these wages.

Carl was a huge favorite of our sponsors. No one worked harder, and it showed.

The Reagan administration raked Israel through the coals for attacking Iraq's nuclear reactor. It voted with the

UN Security Council to strongly condemn the action.

The resolution urged Israel to pay damages to Iraq. I wouldn't hold my breath.

Justice Potter Stewart decided to step down from the U.S. Supreme Court.

Women's groups came up with a list of favorite candidates. President Reagan said he was always on the lookout for someone to possibly become the court's first female member.

Presidential spokesman David Gergen said, "What we're looking for is the best qualified person—man or woman."

June 21, 1981

We ran the all-time worst lead ever. It was so awful I won't tell you who wrote it.

The story was about an assistant district attorney in Rockland County who was killed in a car crash Friday afternoon.

The lead: *There's a job opening in the DA's office this morning.*

You couldn't make this shit up.

You'd never know former President Gerald Ford was an outstanding athlete in his day. I mean, he played football at Michigan. How good was that?

Now he makes news for his athletic foibles. For the second time, he bopped a spectator with a golf ball during a celebrity tournament. He beaned another spectator four years ago on the same course.

June 22, 1981

Mark David Chapman admitted he murdered John Lennon.

He took a plea deal so he could get twenty to life in prison rather than the usual twenty-five to life. He's to be sentenced August 24.

I'll always remember the night of December 8, working in the newsroom with Eti and the gang when shortly before eleven a bulletin came over the AP wire that Lennon had been shot outside his home at the Dakota in New York City.

The reports came in rapid-fire. He was on his way to the hospital. He was there. Then he was dead.

Being a daytime radio station, we weren't on the air to report any of this. All we could do was call the news director for suggestions on how to cover this in the morning.

Obviously, all we could get was man on the street reaction along with shit from gun control advocates and the like. Over at WRNW, the station was wall-to-wall Lennon and the Beatles.

Other than Beatles covers, the music was strictly from the group.

Gary Axelbank and I spoke at length on the air during his show. He later told me he saved the tape.

June 23, 1981

Dave Saviet told me Yvonne Mobley got a job at WRKS. That was a very popular urban music station in the big city. Good for her. Maybe I'll be next.

Not there, of course, but somewhere.

June 24, 1981

Who said I couldn't predict the news. A Rockland Grand Jury cleared Ramapo Police Officer David Lamond of any wrongdoing in the yarmulke shooting.

Rockland DA Kenneth Gribetz read a statement after the decision. "Thirteen witnesses testified. They included civilians, police officers, and Officer Lamond. The grand jury made the determination not to charge Officer Lamond with any violation of the law.

Lamond spoke briefly after the decision. "I'm relieved, —overwhelmingly relieved."

Mixing celebrities and heartwarming stories was a staple of local news. That was especially true when the celebrity was a local legend like Helen Hayes.

She was so much of a legend that a local physical rehab hospital was named for her. Miss Hayes donated much of her time there for the past thirty-seven years.

Today, she went to the medical center to listen to a prodigy of hers play the organ.

Lee Donovan had a severe case of cerebral palsy. Miss Hayes was alternately excited and moved when she watched him play.

"God bless you. Oh, Lee, you're a wonder man. Isn't it great to see Lee learn that song especially for me? It makes me choked up. Believe me, I could weep when I see him but I wouldn't think of doing so."

She compared working at the hospital with working in the acting profession.

"It's the one place where I get immediate response. You get the feeling whether you succeeded or not immediately on stage, and in this place where you walk in and know the people are happy and well cared for."

June 26, 1981

Eti and I went to the Office in Nyack to hear Ron Carter and whatever band he put together. I made every effort to expand Eti's musical universe.

Carter was a bassist who had appeared on hundreds of albums. You probably heard his name mentioned in what was a pet peeve of mine.

Why did DJs insist on naming every musician on jazz albums? It wasn't done anywhere else. You never heard, "That was Peter Wolf, Seth Justman, Danny Klein, J. Geils, and Magic Dick" when the jock played the J. Geils band.

So why was it done on jazz records? Was it necessary to tell us who played the skin flute along with the drummer, percussionist, saxophonist, and keyboard player?

Boring.

The Office was owned by someone who also fancied himself as a drummer. I forgot his name. He insisted on playing with every band he brought in. Most of the bands weren't very good, but Carter was a legend in his own right.

You could see he was getting progressively irritated as the "house drummer" kept missing the beat.

I was sure we'd never see Carter again. Not at the Office, anyway.

June 27, 1981

Police in Atlanta arrested a suspect in connection with the killing of a young black man. Cops believed Wayne Williams may be the person they had been looking for in the recent deaths of twenty-seven others.

If you were a ticket holder for future shows at the Coachlight Dinner Theater, you were shit out of luck.

The district attorney threatened to get involved, but we'll see. If the people who owned the theater had no money, they had no money for ticket holders.

June 28, 1981

Lori was munching on a cookie when she told me one of our biggest sponsors leaned on Bob Marvin to spike one of our stories.

The King Oil Company was a home delivery service. They paid WRKL about fifteen thousand dollars a year. We found out the company illegally buried a number of oil tanks on its property, so we ran with it.

"Marvin told them he couldn't interfere with the news, so they dropped the account."

"Good for him."

June 29, 1981

The Ninth Judicial District was still unable to find a free lawyer for Belton Brims.

In court, the accused murderer told State Supreme Court Judge Isaac Rubin, "I don't appreciate you sending me these rinky-dink Rockland lawyers to represent me. Maybe you can get Clarence Darrow."

This fucking idiot was serious. Brims also contacted William Kunstler. Rubin told Brims he could represent himself, with Conrad Lynn as his advisor.

Lynn was still trying to get out of the case. At several points, reporters and spectators laughed at Brims' high-jinks.

As we filed out, DA Kenneth Gribetz muttered, "You wouldn't be laughing if you saw what this brutal fucking animal did to the Sohns."

Prosecutors working the John Youman's murder case were dealt a blow. One of their key witnesses died.

They knew Jacob Conklin was on his way out. That was why they set up a videotape in his room at Good Samaritan Hospital in Suffern. Conklin died of cancer and other ailments before they could roll the tape.

Conklin lived with Youman's mother for thirty-five years.

He was expected to come up with negatives about Youman's personality during that time.

Pretrial hearings had begun. This was where the prosecution tried to get a judge to allow as much evidence as possible and the defense to do the opposite.

June 30, 1981

Here was something I never knew:

If you sold pills that were legal, such as caffeine or vitamins, but misrepresented them as amphetamines, you'd be charged as a drug dealer selling the more potent drug.

That was what a Suffern storeowner faced.

Police said dozens of kids who thought they were getting Black Beauties or Quaaludes ended up with something legal like No-Doze.

The district attorney said the investigation and arrest came after his office received complaints from disgruntled consumers.

If you didn't believe the public was forgiving when it came to crooked judges, you will now. Either the voters were forgiving, or they needed a place to get their tickets fixed.

Clarkstown Town Justice Robert Maidman was suspended about two years ago for just that—fixing tickets. He was one of three candidates who just won nominations for his old job back. Even if he lost in the general election, he'd be okay.

After his suspension, he was kept on as a deputy town attorney. The ticket fixer would be allowed to hold on to that post no matter what happened.

July 2, 1981

Lady Di added an unconventional twist to her wedding vows.

Diana Spencer won't promise to obey Prince Charles when they marry July 29. On the bright side, she did say she'd pledge to love and comfort him.

The Archbishop of Canterbury said leaving out the traditional word *obey* was the couple's decision.

July 3, 1981

"It's a disgrace the way the county treats deceased veterans." That was from one of my hotline callers.

"The veterans' cemetery is overrun with weeds. Many of the old headstones are broken. What's worse, some graves have sunk three feet. You'd think the county ought to get in and make the cemetery a place we would be proud of instead of the way it looks. The burial commissioner told me funding is so low, it took five years to get water in there."

I promised to check it out.

But first, I headed to Nyack to meet Sam Felder and talk with those supposedly in the know about Gribetz's targeting of the Zada family.

"I have a couple of friends waiting with the information that's necessary for you to go forward. They're in the vicinity of the church."

There was a Fourth of July festival going on, so it was pretty crowded on Broadway.

We headed from Main Street, south to a big red church on Broadway that had been around since the Civil War. Felder seemed nervous. He was fast-talking me about his ride to Sing Sing.

"I was a kid. Two guards brought me there. Both of them made me suck their dicks. I was scared shitless. That's why I did it.

"I survived. I read a lot. I learned to play chess. I played regularly with one of the guys who offed Malcolm X."

"Did you beat him?"

"Never, he was too good."

We got to the church, and there was no one there other

than the throngs of tourists up from New York City for a day in the country on a holiday weekend.

"Wait here. I'll find out where these guys are."

I'll admit I started to get a bit paranoid. Not leery. *Who were these fucking guys?* I started to scan the rooftops. Some of these so-called friends were killers. I'm sure they didn't give a shit about me. If you love news, you gladly take risks. Unfortunately, I sensed there was no story here, that I was just wasting a shitload of my time.

Felder showed up.

"I can't locate them. Can you stick around? We'll get coffee."

"I have to get back to the station. I have a shitload of work to do and holiday weekends are a bitch. Maybe I'll get lucky and someone will blow his fingers off playing with cherry bombs. It happens every year."

"OK. I'll find out what happened."

"Keep in touch. Better yet, call Len Maniace at the *Journal News*. He'll love the story, and once it's in the paper, we'll jump on it."

Everything seemed to go up but my embarrassingly paltry salary. First, the post office wanted to up the price of a stamp to twenty cents. We could be seeing toll hikes on some of the area bridges.

The Port Authority wanted to raise tolls on its four bridges and two tunnels to two dollars for a round trip. The money would supposedly go toward buying new buses.

Finally, subway fares may be going up to seventy-five cents soon. It's sixty cents right now.

Lori Siegel talked to Rockland commuters so she could

file a couple of reports. "It doesn't hit me very well because my salary didn't go up that much."

"I don't believe the service is that good."

"The subway isn't worth sixty cents, so anything more is a rip-off."

"I've got to get around, I don't have much choice."

"Higher fares will drive people back to their automobiles."

I looked at the bright side. At least my toilet paper and cookies are free.

July 5, 1981

Toll collectors on the Garden State Parkway walked off the job. They made about eight dollars an hour. The collectors were offered ten and a half dollars this year and twelve next year.

That wasn't bad just for sticking your hand out. Sadly, that was more than even our news director made. Forget about the rest of us. That wasn't counting all the stuff we did for free, including the Felder fiasco.

They picked the busy Fourth of July weekend to strike. It was one way to stick it to supervisors and administrators who had to man the booths on their holiday. We knew traffic to the Jersey Shore was heavy.

Supervisors claimed everything was moving smoothly. There was a good reason for it. Most motorists breezed through the toll booths without paying the usual quarter.

Thirty-eight

Up, Up, and Away

I had covered some unique stories in my time, but nothing like this.

How about a balloon race from up in a balloon? It sounded like a good idea at the time. The truth be told, I was scared shitless of heights.

When I was very young, we lived in Brooklyn. My mother would take my sister, brother, and me on the roof of our apartment building to get some sun. Every once in a while, she'd yell, "Don't go near the edge, you'll fall."

I remember ambulance people carrying a next-door neighbor on a stretcher. He had just died. When I asked what happened, my mother said, "He fell off the roof."

In retrospect, I didn't know if that was true. Still, that warning stuck with me. So here I was at the Nanuet Mall with more than twenty hot air balloons ready to go.

I might have been on the verge of chickening out—my mind was blank. I was assigned a pilot named Jack O'Connor from Deerfield Beach, Florida.

Fellow first-timer Michael Belay also came. O'Connor gave us a quick briefing. "You only have vertical control up and down. The winds will change about five degrees every thousand feet that you go up."

I thought, "A thousand feet? Wasn't that the height of the Empire State Building? Fuck this."

O'Connor went on, "The wind will change about one hundred eighty degrees at around four to five thousand feet."

Five thousand feet? Shit. That's a mile high.

"This is a hare and hound race where competitors follow the lead balloon, then try to be the one that lands closest to it. Let's go."

I felt this tremendous pang in my stomach. At least there was nothing in my underwear. Not yet, anyway. In the military, they say, "Keep a tight asshole" if there are bullets flying. Now I knew what that meant.

At the moment of truth, I told myself sternly, "Be a man." And I clumsily climbed into the basket.

I know many women who would have hopped into the balloon without breaking a sweat. Eti was one. She'd have no problem.

However, "be a man" worked for me.

The basket didn't go up to my waist. I held tightly to the rope that led to the canvas over us. We took off like a shot.

Shit.

As we ascended, I was surprised at how loud the jet or burner or whatever it was sounded as it fired hot air into the balloon. I had always imagined floating in the air in peaceful silence with only the sound of my heart beating heavily.

The other passenger spoke as we floated three hundred feet over the mall. A dozen balloons were below us.

"It looks beautiful. Never saw a sight like this. Real nice."

He never muttered another word.

O'Connor tried to calm me down a little. He must have sensed I was a bit nervous. Maybe it was the white knuckles on the rope that gave me away.

"We're gonna watch this weather awful close. We've got a lot of bad weather around us, but we're in a good spot right here. If it doesn't deteriorate, we'll be all right."

Then he gave a reality check.

"If you get into those cumulous clouds, it'll suck you right up. We've got to stay clear of them. You'll get tremendous turbulence."

We got a bird's-eye view of Rockland at only seventeen hundred feet heading east to the Hudson River. Then it was time to land.

"The most dangerous part is tearing up the balloon if you go into the trees."

I kept my arm crocked around the rope as I tape recorded my interviews. O'Connor laughed nervously.

"Another warning, when we land, keep your knees bent and get low and hold on to something. Don't fall out of the basket. If we lose a passenger, the loss of weight will force us to shoot up again. The force of nature dictates where we land."

I continued to hold on to the rope. There would be no pulling it out of my tightly clenched fist.

We literally scraped the treetops of a wooded area behind an industrial building off Route 303 in Orangetown.

I felt this indescribable exhilaration as I jumped out of the gondola.

"Holy shit, I did it." And no racing stripes in my underpants.

I drove back to the radio station and put my stories together.

Thirty-nine

Armed, Very Dangerous, and on the Lam

July 6, 1981

So here I was, working really late into the wee small hours of the morning putting the morning news together, which I was to anchor because of the holiday weekend when the police scanner blared an all points bulletin, "We have an escapee from the Rockland County Jail. Belton Brims is six feet, two hundred forty pounds. He sports a neatly trimmed afro and is wearing a tee shirt, shorts, and a stocking cap. Brims was held on two counts of murder. He's considered armed and very dangerous."

Every one of our staffers was called. This is a story we'd work on intensely. Forget about sleeping.

Rockland DA Kenneth Gribetz said investigators visited

dozens of known Brims hangouts already.

"We've spoken to friends, acquaintances, and relatives. Roadblocks were set up near the jail as soon as we knew he was gone. We have state police tracking dogs sniffing out his trail. Right now, we have nothing."

I had never heard Sheriff Ray Lindemann this angry. Remember, the escape came on his watch. We got him on the phone.

"We've searched the building. We've searched the grounds. We're searching cars. We have roadblocks out for anybody. He may have manned a car to go out on the road. All county police departments have been notified. That includes Bergen County."

"Lord knows where he would go. I wish I had his mind. I'm no Dick Tracy. I wish I knew how it happened. My orders were he don't move unless he has two or three men with him. I don't know how a prisoner gets out of a locked cell. I'm going to find out. I'm damned sure I'll find out, I'll tell you that. He had to go through a skylight via a ladder. The skylight was locked. We found the lock had been broken."

What made matters worse for Lindemann was that he faced what had become a tough election in November. His opponent, Thomas Goldrick, didn't wait before calling on Lindemann to resign.

"I'm so upset and every citizen of Rockland County should feel the same way.

This is the fourteenth escape in the past ten years. We have a sheriff who's responsible for a jail and one of the most vicious killers has been allowed to break out. I'm just sick and tired of the excuses that the sheriff uses."

July 7, 1981

If Belton Brims was hiding in the woods, he'd run into the millions of gypsy moths that were eating their way through Rockland County.

They also left behind tens of thousands of cocoons in trees that were most visible on the parkway as well as on major roads throughout.

Ugly.

Now we learned how Brims got out. Sheriff Lindemann said the escapee somehow got his hands on a hacksaw.

"The last time Brims was seen was at eleven thirty Sunday night. He was reported missing at eight Monday morning. He went through locked doors. He made it to the fourth floor skylight and broke the lock. There were five corrections officers who made certain the doors to all cells, including Brims' on the jail's third tier, were securely locked during the night bed check. We're talking to them as well as several inmates. That's as far as we know now."

Rockland Jail Superintendent Elijah Coleman said officers entered Brims' locked cell in the morning when he didn't respond to them.

"They found Brims' bed stuffed with sheets and papers to simulate a sleeping inmate. He had severed three bars with a hacksaw and soaped the metal to hide the marks. The fire escape door was left open to aid ventilation. The jail gets extremely hot at night. Brims went to the fourth tier, climbed a metal ladder to an interior skylight, broke the lock, and made his way to the roof. A small amount of blood was found there. He dropped twenty feet to a lower roof and ran to a point where he jumped to the ground. We believe Brims is still somewhere in the county. He may be on foot or he may have taken a car."

Brims' lawyer, Conrad Lynn, said he doubts his would-be client will be taken alive.

"He has been convicted of a number of crimes. He's a man that we have to be concerned about."

Sheryl Sohn's lawyer, Patrick Burke, said his client may get her wish to be tried alone. "Brims is a tough-looking fellow. That might have influenced a jury against her."

All this had county lawmakers wringing their hands again about overcrowding at the fifty-two-year-old jail.

On a national note, President Reagan nominated Sandra Day O'Connor for the U.S. Supreme Court.

The Arizona appeals judge got high praise from both sides of the aisle.

July 8, 1981

We got an update on the Brims search from Sheriff Lindemann. "We have no house-to-house search going on. We had some information and hit a couple of places. That was it. We had a report of a black man walking up Old Hempstead Road in an all-white neighborhood, so we went up to see him. The description was the same as Brims, but it wasn't him, so we let him go."

July 9, 1981

I finally got my court appearance in Queens over that incident I told you about at the Whitestone Bridge where I took off because I was getting my balls broken by a cop who held onto my registration.

Eti came with me.

The complaining officer was a no-show. That was lucky for me because in traffic cases, no matter what the cop said, the court took his word for it. That was how the system worked 100 percent of the time.

That "innocent until proven guilty" propaganda we were fed as we grew up was just that—propaganda.

The judge wanted to set a new date, but I chimed in, "Can't we have this adjudicated today?"

"OK, not guilty."

Eti chuckled. It turns out it wasn't because of the judge's decision. She said she didn't realize I knew any big words.

For the second time in little over half a year, the third accused murderer in the Sohn case, James Sheffield was in police custody and released.

Sheffield was arrested in Toronto on an unrelated charge and fingerprinted by Canadian authorities. According to the *Journal News*, the prints were handed over to the FBI. Instead of checking them through their computer system immediately, the agency waited until the day Sheffield was released.

He was in a Toronto jail for two weeks in June. From there, he was deported to the United States and ended up in either Chicago or Detroit.

You remember Sheffield was arrested by North Plainfield, New Jersey, police two hours after the Sohn murders. He was charged with violating a borough ordinance that made it unlawful to be in a public park at night.

Lori Siegel called the FBI to find out why they waited so

long. They blamed Rockland for the delay in printing copies of a circular that had mug shots and fingerprints of the three suspects.

Hunger striker Joe McDonnell became the fourth to die of starvation at Maze Prison. Irish Bishops called the strike evil.

McDonnell's death was followed by violence in Belfast.

The two convicted murderers in the Paula Bohovesky case were given twenty-five years to life in prison. Joseph La-Barbera and Robert McCain stood ashen faced before Judge Harry Edelstein as he imposed the maximum sentence.

Two men were in critical condition following the crash of their small plane where the Garden State Parkway met the New York State Thruway.

We sent Tim Scheld. "We learned that a marine veterinarian and his pilot were testing their specially equipped single engine Cessna when it lost power shortly after takeoff from the Ramapo Valley airport. They tried to land on the thruway shortly after three in the afternoon. The plane fell short and burst into flames. Dr. Jay Hyman was planning to look for narwhales during a summer expedition to the Arctic Circle. The sophisticated whale-finding equipment was worth an estimated one hundred thousand dollars."

July 10, 1981

If nothing else, the Brims escape served as a catalyst for building a new jail. The county's planning and public works committee agreed to hire an architect.

Judge Harry Edelstein said he had a more practical idea.

"For two hundred dollars, this county could have had a hand detector for anybody coming into the jail or for any major trial where you need security. The legislature kicked the idea around, talked about it, and did nothing. For two hundred bucks, they probably could have gotten federal money for a number of hand detectors."

As far as the Brims search, Sheriff Ray Lindemann said it was centering on the "hill" section of Spring Valley near where the fugitive lived with his family.

"We know he didn't have any money. That's why we think he's still around. We've been working on every angle we possibly can. Everything will come out sooner or later. I can't say truthfully that somebody worked with him. We're following every lead, every telephone call."

Forty

Cold Case Arguments

Opening arguments finally began in the Youman's murder trial. I say, finally, because the crime happened in 1952.

Most of the people at the radio station weren't born yet. This became a national story with reporters from *Esquire* and the *New York Times* joining the locals.

The best coverage was being done by the *Journal News*. The paper had been on top of this through the pre-trial hearings.

Assistant DA Frank Phillips told the jury the case against Youmans was based on circumstantial evidence. He could say that again.

"What you'll hear is testimony from family members and acquaintances who heard the defendant confess on numerous occasions to killing Ramapo Town Clerk Robert Nugent and Banker Charles Simpson."

To rehash, their bodies were found sprawled near their vehicle in the woods three miles west of Tuxedo on October 26, 1952. They had been shot-gunned execution style in the head and back. The two had set out for an afternoon hunt the previous day in Sterling Forest between Tuxedo in Orange County and Sloatsburg. This was two weeks before deer season began. The carcass of a buck was between them.

Authorities speculated at the time the pair was killed by a poacher after he happened upon them. Taking deer for venison was a mini industry at that time. It even had a name: deer jacking.

It was one of Nugent's jobs to hand out hunting licenses. He may have recognized his killer.

John Youmans worked in one of the area's iron mines at that time. He became a handyman and construction worker when the mines closed.

When the trial began, he was suffering from mouth cancer and other ailments. He didn't look good. He was still recovering from his latest mouth surgery. His face was marked with skin grafts. His jaw was swollen.

Phillips said Youmans was picked up in February after his sister broke what she said was a twenty-eight-year vow of silence she made to her mother.

"Several younger brothers and sisters were at the mother's house at the time of the killing. Youmans lived next door with his former common law wife, Harriet Marsh. The children living there are going to come in and testify about things that stayed in their mind. They will tell you that the defendant came home bloodied and told his mother, 'I just shot Bob Nugent.'"

Defense lawyer Seymour Greenblatt spoke briefly. "That

kind of testimony isn't proof. The prosecution has no evidence to prove guilt beyond a reasonable doubt. There are no eyewitnesses, no murder weapon, and no motive to link Youmans to the crime. Both victims were found with their jewelry and wallets intact.

Forty-one

A Bad Place to Take a Leak

There was a freak death on the Tappan Zee Bridge. Three men from upstate New York pulled their car over in the middle of the span heading into Rockland from Westchester to relieve themselves.

Nineteen-year-old Andrew Matheson slipped on the girder and fell into the Hudson River. His body was found almost immediately.

We still needed more stories for the desk.

Luckily, Linda Winikow called with a rant about dismantling the MTA. The state senator said the county was getting screwed because it put money into the MTA and got nothing whatsoever in return.

"The only way we can end this chaos is to start over again, but the state is unwilling to do it. It's like a whale. The mouth of the whale is the MTA. It has an insatiable appetite. It wants more and more money, and it's going into that bottomless pit."

There were three usable sound bites here. Realistically, I had a better chance of running for governor than she had of ending the MTA.

Speaking of which, Mario Cuomo said he'll probably run for governor next year. He said it wasn't hard to find reasons for him not to run.

I wonder what this did to Winikow's dream of running for lieutenant governor. It would be plausible, but only if she put her money on the right horse.

A state Supreme Court judge put a halt to a zoning law that was designed to relax enforcement of housing violations by the Vishnitz Hasidic community in Monsey.

The area was zoned for one-family housing. The ultra orthodox group took it upon themselves to turn scores of dwellings into multifamily units to the dismay of people who were already living there. The town went ahead and changed the zoning to allow the multifamily units. The judge wanted the town to find a better way to do it.

July 11, 1981

Since I'd be doing some of the Youmans trial, I decided to drive to the Ringwood/Sloatsburg area where he lived and worked in the 1950s. Maybe I could get some insights and maybe some comments on tape.

It was something we all did. WRKL wasn't a local news giant by accident. Everyone went the extra mile.

The iron mining industry was shut several years after Youmans worked there.

The Ford plant in nearby Mahwah, New Jersey, used the site to dump tens of thousands of pounds of paint sludge.

The lead-based stew also contained arsenic, benzene, and other carcinogenic chemicals.

Hundreds of people living in the region suffered from asthma and various types of cancers. It was probably the reason Youmans and a key witness who just died battled cancer.

Going there was a bit of a mistake. There were many dirt roads off the beaten path. The potholes were deep enough to bend the axel of the rental car I was still using thanks to Bob Marvin. I could have been in Appalachia. Some of the homes were made out of plywood; others were old trailers.

A dam was planned in a few years that would put all these structures underwater. I got hostile looks from virtually everyone. I began thinking of the "Deliverance" theme.

I wasn't getting out of my car. At this point, I wondered whether I'd be on the wrong end of target practice. I thought I better haul ass before I ended up like Nugent and Simpson.

Forty-two

Synagogue Bombed

July 12, 1981

A pipe bomb explosion damaged a New City synagogue.

Police said it was a two-inch-diameter pipe bomb with a length of six to seven inches.

Rabbi Cohen of the New City Jewish Center pointed out quite a bit of damage. "On one side of our sanctuary, the windows were all blown out. Part of the ceiling outside is blown out. It's unfortunate that something like this could happen in 1981 in New City or anywhere else. I'm sure we have plenty of enemies. I'm also sure it's just sick people."

Some members of the synagogue were beyond outraged:

"We're going to deal with them. I think the police know who they are."

"We're going to set an example."

"I don't want another case like the one in Spring Valley

two years ago where a guy got off with five years probation for desecrating a synagogue with swastikas. Now we're talking about pipe bombs. Next time people are going to get hurt."

DA Kenneth Gribetz held a news conference. "It appeared to be a homemade but powerful device that blew out eleven windows and caused structural damage as well as interior damage. That's due to the fragmentation of the device. It doesn't appear to be a professional job, but we're not ruling anything out."

Forty-three

Heavy Falling Out

July 13, 1981

There were points where the prosecution's key witness against accused double murderer John Youmans could hardly be understood between her sobs.

Billie Kessler was John Youmans' sister. She told the jury she remembered that day in October well. "John got his gun and told us he was going deer hunting. Three hours later, he returned looking scared to death. He had blood on his shirt. John asked if the police were there. He told us he shot a deer. Then he said he shot Bob Nugent. He told me Nugent begged for his life, that he kicked him down and shot him. He later said he killed Simpson. He told us if anyone asks, he never left the house. He went upstairs to clean his gun. He left in his car to get rid of it. For some time, he said he couldn't sleep because he couldn't get Nugent's face out of his mind."

Philips asked why she waited so long to come forward.

"I promised my mother I'd never tell."

Youmans' wife, Lucille, held a Bible as she and three of their children sat behind the defendant.

Clarkstown police learned more about the synagogue bombing. Lt. Ronald Purnom said remnants of the bomb were tagged.

"They've been sent to the alcohol, tobacco, and firearms laboratory in Rockville, Maryland. The tests will show what the bomb was made of and what it was filled with. We're working on the assumption that a group of juveniles were responsible. We have a few leads, including names."

July 14, 1981

Billie Kessler had a tough day under cross-examination.

The sister of the accused killer admitted having a homosexual relationship with Youmans' current wife.

Mrs. Kessler also admitted an incestuous episode with her brother John when she was fifteen. It landed her in the Hudson Girls Training School until she was eighteen.

She also spoke of bad blood between members of her family. They included threats and harassment charges.

Perhaps most important, she told the jury John Youmans confessed to the murders at ten in the morning. State police investigators put the time of death at three that afternoon.

Forty-four

Free Cheese Handouts
for Newsies

My brother and sister-in-law were getting worried.

As I wrote before, she worked for Pan Am. She had been saying for years that the airline was going down the toilet. Workers had been taking pay and benefit cuts. The union wasn't doing shit for them.

What used to be the largest air carrier in the world suspended all service at Newark and La Guardia airports.

Pan Am's president said the airline would be concentrating its operation in New York into and out of Kennedy Airport. It included cutting back service between the northeast and the southern United States.

In a news release, the president said he was taking "aggressive and positive action to position Pan Am geographically in order to fully capitalize on trade route markets."

In other words, he didn't have a fucking clue.

I know it was bad form to write "good news, bad news" stories, but this was different.

The Reagan administration cut thirty-eight billion dollars from social service programs. If you were rich and free of a conscience, that would be good news.

The real good news was everyone in our news department will become eligible for a government cheese handout the Reagan administration announced that'll begin next year. We were making so little, that we were lumped in with welfare and food stamp recipients along with seniors on social security.

The real bad news was it wasn't really cheese. It would be something called cheese food—whatever that is.

We had a list of places where we would be able to pick up our bounty. I loved working here. I just couldn't afford it. *Uh, thank you Bob Marvin*. A special thank you went out to the losers who shit-canned my resumes. You missed out on a kick-ass reporter who never quit working.

I gave Dan Duprey the news about the free cheese giveaway. That led us into our usual complaining about how our careers were tanking. We were killing ourselves and weren't getting anywhere. This sucked.

He said it reminded him of an old joke. "There was this sperm cell. He wanted to be the one that fertilized the egg, but he realized it wouldn't be easy. So he exercised nonstop. He swam. He hiked. He jogged. He ran. He did sit-ups and bench presses. He jumped rope and did everything a sperm cell could do and then some. At the same time, he noticed the competition lounging around. They floated in the pool. They drank lemonade. They laughed and had a good old time. No one worked. 'This is going to be easy.' Then the Big Moment came. Like a flash, he was out almost immediately. He was in front. Then he was way ahead. Finally, he was out of sight. Moments later, he swam frantically back to the pack. 'Go back,' he screamed. 'Go back. It's a blowjob.'"

God, I hope my career doesn't turn out this way.

Look, I took the risk. I should give it time. For the most part, I'm enjoying the journey. I love every minute of covering news. I have a passion for it.

Besides, where else could I get free tee shirts with WRKL logos on them and free toilet paper?

I got to meet former peace activist Daniel Berrigan. The former priest was in Rockland to speak to the Irish Arts Forum. He called for a united Ireland. I didn't know how peaceful that would be.

You may remember he came into the public eye when he poured blood on draft records in the '60s.

Instead of clerical garb, Berrigan wore brown corduroy pants and a plaid shirt. "The plight of the prisoners in Long Kesh won't be solved in Ireland or in Britain, but here in the United States. Irish people here must become activist."

July 15, 1981

The prosecution brought out a string of witnesses who'd implicate John Youmans in the double murders. Next was Billie Kessler's ex-husband.

Joseph Van Houton said he was a friend of Youmans since 1945.

"We often hunted together. On several occasions while they were drinking together, John said he had shot Nugent. Sometimes he'd brag there was a reward out for him."

A brother of the defendant told the jury how John Youmans took a shot at him after the two got into a fistfight. He also accused Youmans of raping his wife.

July 16, 1981

Casper Jones was the latest of Youmans' former brothers-in-law to take the stand. Jones testified when he and the defendant were arrested in connection with an alleged rape in 1959, Youmans told fellow inmates if he wasn't worried about killing people, he wasn't going to worry about a rape charge.

What happened with that rape charge wasn't disclosed in court? Jones also testified that in the mid 1950s when he and Youmans were working on a construction project, he told a bulldozer operator who had splashed mud on him to stop or you'll be under the mud. "I'll plant you. I've planted others."

He told the jury Youmans once knocked him through a window during an argument.

A tentative deal was reached in the toll collectors' strike. Now they're really going to make much more than us at the radio station. Their hands are expected to be seen sticking out of their respective booths beginning sometime tomorrow.

Bloodhounds apparently picked up a scent of Belton Brims. A tracking team of canines from the state police followed the scent to a vacant apartment on Bethune Boulevard in the "hill" section of Spring Valley.

Rich Mendelson lived nearby, so he joined the search. He caught up with the sheriff's patrol chief, James Kralick. He was in charge of the dragnet.

"We've certainly received plenty of tips that he's still in the county. They've proved fruitless, but there's still plenty of action that way. I'd say it's fifty-fifty he's still here."

Forty officers and a police helicopter combed the area. There were reports Brims was seen two times by police during the search.

"We secured the buildings. We searched the woods behind them. No cars were allowed into Bethune Boulevard, and all cars coming out were searched. That includes inside the trunks."

The two-and-a-half-hour manhunt was called off at around eight thirty this morning.

Harry Chapin was killed on the Long Island Expressway today. You may remember him for *Taxi* and *Cats in the Cradle*.

I remember Chapin raised millions of dollars for hunger groups. When I was at WBAB on Long Island, Chapin came in and gave a free mini concert in order to raise money. He was a great guy—no ego.

He had a history of traffic violations that ended with his license being revoked. Witnesses said the thirty-eight-year-old singer and songwriter was weaving in and out of traffic lanes.

He pulled in front of a tractor-trailer and got clipped. His car burst into flames. The truck driver cut Chapin's seatbelt and yanked him out of the car. Sadly, it wasn't in time to save him.

July 17, 1981

Another one of John Youmans' sisters implicated her brother in the double murders of two men in 1952.

Genevieve McClellan testified in 1967, her brother was very drunk and crying when he came to her.

"He said he needed to be sent to a psychiatric hospital. He said he still hears Bob Nugent moaning and groaning."

Westchester found a controversial way to alleviate its jail overpopulation problem. It's letting a bunch of hard core criminals out.

Some of those let go included a man charged with a double murder, a man accused of sodomizing an eleven-year-old boy, and an accused burglar described by the prosecutor as a habitual criminal and a thief.

Guards armed with rifles stood on the roof of the Westchester County Jail as nearly sixty inmates were brought one at a time with their lawyers into the gym to plead their case.

The judge sat under a basketball hoop. I sat in the stands with the other news people.

A promise to hold these hearings helped end last weekend's seventy-two-hour rampage by three hundred inmates who caused a half-million-dollar damage. They complained about excessive bail, overly long waits for trials, and juries made up of mostly rich white people.

Inmate Sherman Jenkins was granted twenty thousand dollars bail. He was the one accused of a double homicide last year. His legal aid lawyer said Jenkins had strong roots in the community.

An accused burglar had his bail reduced to almost nothing. James Meyers's lawyer said his client was a lifelong Yonkers resident. The Westchester Assistant DA who opposed the bail pointed out that Meyers spent more time in jail than he did in Yonkers.

"Meyers has no roots in Yonkers other than he knows everyone's houses and how to get into them."

July 19, 1981

Carl Nathe was in early to do several pieces on the Rockland All-County baseball team. It's all we had since the major league players were still on strike.

"Suffern is completely dominating this team. They have five players and their coach. Tony DeFrancesco was drafted by the California Angels. Another real good one is Walter Weiss. He's a four-something hitter, and he's only a junior."

We learned the radio station had a problem with the septic system. The biggest clue was the Porto-San in the back next to the parking lot.

Steve Possell was really pissed.

He had to feel his way around that smelly shit house until something was done to the lavatories.

"This place smells awful. The urinal is wet. I'd never sit on the toilet."

What was worse was that Bob Marvin was in no rush. His goal was to find someone who'd fix the problem in exchange for free commercials.

July 21, 1981

It was the defense's turn in the Youmans trial. Youmans' former common-law wife told the jury the defendant helped his mother move to a new home on the day of the shootings.

Other witnesses said they never heard Youmans say he killed anyone.

Conrad Lynn was told he'll face a contempt citation if he continued to refuse to represent Belton Brims. Judge John Gallucci wanted Lynn to represent Brims "in absentia."

Lynn decided to hire Bill Kunstler who spoke to the hoard of media people who surrounded him.

"So the pretense here is if Mr. Lynn is sitting there in court, even with Mr. Brims absent that Mr. Brims will be adequately, legally protected. I think it's a fallacy, and I think they're trying to take this lawyer who has practiced more years than most of us have been alive and make him subject to the contempt provision. I told Judge Gallucci I would have Mr. Lynn write him a letter explaining why he's not appearing. He doesn't represent Mr. Brims, and he never has except formally by court order. He has been repudiated by Mr. Brims."

In the meantime, Sheryl Sohn's lawyer, Patrick Burke, argued to have pretrial hearings closed to the news media.

Tim Scheld got on Burke's good side. Scheld played ice hockey on St. Francis's national champion team last year.

Now he was showing Burke's son how to improve his skating skills at a local rink.

Burke said the hearings will center on confessions his client made to both Spring Valley police and state troopers from Middletown in Orange County. You remember Sohn was arrested on January 14 while staying at a friend's house.

"She was arraigned the next day and charged with masterminding the robbery and murder of her parents. My client was promised immunity from prosecution if she promised to cooperate with police by making the statements. These statements are the basis for her indictment. They were made unlawfully and should be banned from actual testimony. Without the statements, there isn't much of a case."

I chime in, "The truth is, she confessed."

Burke shot back, "I don't deal with truth. I deal with facts."

WRKL and the Journal News brought in attorneys to argue to have the pretrial open to the public. They were turned down.

July 22, 1981

John Youmans told the jury he didn't kill the two hunters he was accused of murdering. He also denied telling anyone he had.

Youmans was pale, gaunt, and toothless as he testified. Despite cancer surgery on his jaw in April, he spoke firmly.

"I never shot them. I never had a reason to shoot anyone. If I did, I don't think I could have lived with it."

Youmans said he worked the overnight shift at a Ringwood, New Jersey, iron mine before helping his mother move from Sloatsburg to Ringwood on the day of the murders. Then he moved his stuff into his mother's old house.

He admitted killing game out of season in order to support his eight sisters and three brothers. He detailed his life as one of twelve children, his drinking problem, and the weekend of the murders.

He told of being questioned by state police on three occasions soon after the shootings. "After the last time, they told me to stick around in the area for a few months in case they had to get back to me. I've been here twenty-eight, going on twenty-nine years."

The defense called ninety-three-year-old William "Teeter" Bill Conklin. He was Sloatsburg's police chief when the murders occurred. He needed a cane to get on the witness stand. Questions had to be shouted at him. He still had a tough time hearing them. The old-timer complained state police made no attempt to secure the crime scene. "Between two thousand and three thousand people tramped through the area for a look at the bodies. I was among the first on the murder scene. I don't know about a poacher committing the murder. I believe the deer found between the two victims had been dead for ten days. The flesh was black as a necktie."

July 23, 1981

We had Dave Peters on the Veterans Cemetery story. "It looks like shit. It's overrun with high grass. No one is maintaining it. Many of the graves go unseeded for months. The gravestones are either sunk into the ground or are crooked or are unmarked."

County Burial Commissioner Tony Lombardi said there

were about thirty-five gravestones that needed to be fixed. "We don't have the equipment or the manpower to do an adequate maintenance job at Rockland's three vet's cemeteries. What we actually need is a full-time crew to take over full responsibility of the cemeteries. That would resolve all these problems. Right now, workers are called to the county jail or anywhere else because they're short. Once you fall behind in a cemetery, there's no catching up."

There could be a link between a woman who was, shall we say, scared stiff when a burglar entered her apartment and the search for Belton Brims.

Seventy-seven-year-old Sonia Fishman called police shortly after three thirty in the afternoon and said someone was in her apartment. Cops said she was very excited. Then the phone went dead.

Witnesses said there were several intruders.

When police arrived, they found the woman unconscious on the floor. She was pronounced dead on arrival at Good Samaritan Hospital in Suffern. Mrs. Fishman had suffered an apparent heart attack.

Roy West was arrested almost immediately. Police said he was friends with Brims.

This led to a search of an apartment complex in Spring Valley by as many as two dozen officers.

July 24, 1981

DA Kenneth Gribetz says there wasn't enough evidence to charge West. "There's no evidence at the present time that the defendant was in the premises. The proceeds of the burglary have been recovered. They weren't in West's possession."

Linda Winikow chewed my ass out for not using her shitty stories the last few times she called.

"Linda, there's a strategy here. I hold them for early morning where there's more than double the audience."

Since I didn't anchor the morning news, I could blame those people for not using her shit.

The state senator didn't buy my story. That was because I burned her in the past. Once when she gave a good story to the paper before she gave it to us, I told her I'm only using her crappy releases on the weekend.

She didn't do that again.

July 25, 1981

Speaking of shitty, Bob Marvin reached a new low, if that was possible. He got one of our engineers, Neil Mazur to dig into the septic tank to find out why the toilets were clogged.

Neil was extremely handy. He and Jeff Baker literally kept the radio station on the air with a high-quality sound not usually found in AM radio. He had this pile of junk car that he somehow kept running. We called it the Neil-mobile.

"I'm standing knee deep in shit and that fucking Marvin kept coming back and standing over me asking if I could tell what was wrong. Yeah, jerk off, there's shit in the pipes. Do you want to suck some of it out? Nothing I could do."

July 27, 1981

The Youmans trial took on a circus atmosphere right off the bat today. The judge allowed the district attorney to present four surprise witnesses to refute Youmans' alibi. Defense lawyer Seymour Greenblatt planned to deliver his summation when he got word.

First, he asked the judge to remove him from the case. When he refused, Greenblatt walked out. He said he didn't feel very well.

The judge replied, "Your present condition appears to be the result of an adverse decision."

The surprise witnesses were retired miners. They told the jury there was no overnight shift as Youmans had testified.

Jean Harris could lose some of her privileges if a weekend brawl at the Bedford Hills Correctional Facility was her fault.

During an altercation, Mrs. Harris and another inmate were found rolling around on the floor. The former school headmistress was punched in the face before they were broken up by corrections guards.

Both women told conflicting stories.

Forty-five

Captured

July 28, 1981

Belton Brims was captured in Selma, Alabama, today. Brims lived in Selma when he was a child.

Police in Rockland had sent a photo of the murder suspect to police there. They also tipped Selma police Brims might be with an old acquaintance named Robert Williams. When cops caught up with Williams in his car, they spotted Brims sitting in the passenger seat.

He was wearing the same stocking cap that was on his Wanted poster. *Smart.*

Selma Police Captain James Foster talked to Lori Siegel over the phone. "Brims tried to get away. He more or less faced a shotgun on him when he ran out from a barbecue area among the houses. He had tried to get under a house, and we were on him real close so he ran on out into the detectives. He quickly gave himself up when he was surrounded by ten police officers. He's very belligerent, especially with law-enforcement officers. He's been appointed an attorney here, and he was even belligerent with him. We learned when we first picked him up that he was wanted for murder in New York, but we had no idea of whom. He's a suspect in the armed robbery of a grocery store where two thousand dollars in cash and food stamps were taken. He's also suspected in a hotel robbery. We did have a lineup as far as both. He may have been in Alabama for as many as three weeks. He told police he took a bus there."

I was at Rockland Sheriff Ray Lindemann's news conference. "The DA and I have been working day and night with my men especially and Spring Valley law enforcement. We all lost a lot of sleep and a lot of time, but I'll tell you something. I'm damned happy he's caught."

Then it was Lindemann being Lindemann.

"We have evidence Brims had been in Rockland up to just a few days ago. The fact Brims is a native of Selma and apparently still has relatives living there, that didn't figure into his capture."

DA Kenneth Gribetz was the most excited. He figured Sheryl Sohn on trial with Brims would be a slam dunk— alone. Who knew?

Dave Peters was at his news conference. "Governor Carey will be asked for the second time in four months to sign extradition papers requesting Brims' return to New York. I'd be pleased if we get him back by August. We hear Brims committed several crimes in Alabama. If they decide to try him and keep him in jail there, it could be quite some time before he's tried here."

Tim Scheld spoke to Sohn lawyer Pat Burke who said, "My first thought was they finally got Belton Brims. My second was I rather doubt we'll have another delay because Sheryl has been awaiting trial since May of this year when the trial date was set. I had asked for separate trials and that was turned down by the court so I can't reapply. I would ask that her trial not be delayed anymore beyond September 1."

We also got man on the street reaction from Spring Valley. "Trust me, I didn't feel any more insecure when he was at large. I'm happy he's apprehended like any person who is wanted by the law. I say how come they didn't watch him in jail? They should have guards there to watch everything. Just Belton being loose didn't affect anything in Spring Valley. It's still dangerous on the streets, especially at nighttime."

July 29, 1981

Thank God for free cheese. Rich Mendelson sold his cookie machine.

He set up a booth in the newly minted Spring Valley Flea Market where he sold brass items. Eti said they were good, so she bought a couple of things we didn't need.

I'm sure the money he got from her more than made up for the cookies I ate.

While we were covering Brims, the rest of the world gave heavy coverage to the wedding of Britain's Prince Charles and Diana, the new Princess of Wales. We had one of our better voices: part-timer Bob Barrera, who put some wire copy on carts. That's it.

Perhaps the most powerful man in New York State history died. Few people today could tell you about Robert Moses. He built virtually every major highway and bridge in the state. He created Jones Beach. Without him, there would be no Triboro or Verrazano Bridges. There would be no Long Island Expressway, Cross Bronx and Van Wyck Expressways, Hutchinson River, Belt, Grand Central, Whitestone, Southern State, or Northern State parkways among others.

He built the United Nations, Lincoln Center, the World's Fair of 1964, and Shea Stadium. If not for him, the Brooklyn Dodgers would still be in New York.

I spoke to Bob Dyson, the chairman of New York's power authority.

"It is very unlikely that anyone else could have built two hydroelectric projects during his time as power authority chairman. The Niagara and St. Lawrence projects are probably New York's most valuable man-made resources. Each year, they save electrical consumers more than one billion dollars. That's more than they cost to build."

Robert Moses was ninety-two.

On a more gritty matter, Diet Doc killer Jean Harris got off the hook for that fight she had with another prisoner last weekend. I called Louis Ganim of the State Department of Corrections.

"Both inmates were credited for the two days they spent on lockup after the incident. That fulfilled their punishment. The penalties were assessed during a hearing by enforcement at Bedford Hills. They didn't determine who was to blame for the incident between Mrs. Harris and a second inmate who wasn't identified. Corrections officers found the two rolling around on the floor. Both were treated for bruises and scratches."

Jean Harris was serving fifteen to life for killing Scarsdale Diet Doctor Herman Tarnower.

July 30, 1981

John Youmans was found not guilty by the jury of nine men and three women. It took them seven hours to reach their verdict.

One juror said there wasn't enough physical evidence. Another said it was a tough case because of the credibility of the witnesses. Speaking outside the courthouse, Youmans said, "I thought I was going to drop when I heard the verdict. I didn't know I had the strength to stand up. I feel strong. I'm anxious to get home and rest."

He had been held on two hundred thousand dollars bail at the Orange County Jail since February 5.

"I'm going to see my doctor tomorrow. Then, I'll go back to work." Youmans began crying. "I love my wife."

We needed an update on Brims. I reached James Sullivan by phone.

He was the district attorney in Selma.

"Well, we're asking for him to be indicted. We're presenting the case. The grand jury will make the decision, but frankly, I believe when you have an ID from the jail lineups, and he was the one who was picked out as the robber, we have a pretty strong little matter against him. As far as an agreement, we'll have to look at our case first to see whether we are going to try him here first or release him back to New

York State. I understand the seriousness of the matter there. However, if we release him to New York, we'll be in the same position New York was in when it comes to extraditing him back down here.

Carl Nathe said the NBA made some rules changes to speed up the game. "They're doing away with the bonus shot. You know, if one team had four fouls in a quarter, the other team had three chances to make two free throws and two chances to make one. Now a two-shot foul will be just that, you get two shots. If you're fouled in the act of shooting and you make the shot, you get one free throw. That's it. Now the players will really have to practice their foul shots."

July 31, 1981

Baseball's fifty-day strike may be over. The players still had to ratify the deal. Word had it the season would resume August ninth with the all-star game in Cleveland. Games would begin the next day.

My guess was most fans would have short memories.

Bob Marvin finally got a Roto-Rooter type company to fix the septic system. I guess the Porto-San got too full.

It got unbelievably raunchy. Poor Steve Possell. He had to hold it in rather than subject himself to the raw sewage that overflowed in our mini shit house.

Marvin walked into the newsroom with his usual dildo-ic look. He carried his cup which had "Master" printed in large letters. He had it hidden in his locked office to prevent someone from using it as a urinal.

I didn't hear him walking through the main office on that carpet the cat sometimes mistook for kitty litter, so there was no escape.

"Hello Bob," he said ominously in his slow nasal whine. "You know, you're probably the strongest man in the newsroom."

I waited for the punch line.

"We need a cesspool trench dug along the side wall where the lavatories are. I don't want to pay an extra ten dollars an hour to someone who doesn't even speak English. How about helping me out?"

"Sure, no problem."

Then, under my breath after he left, "Fuck you, cocksucker."

What was I supposed to do? It wasn't like the phone rang off the hook with job offers.

While I spent two hours digging the trench, I reflected on how I ended up where I was on this day.

Forty-six

How Did I Get Here Anyway?

My goal out of high school was to lead an interesting life. Money wasn't important to me. I began college at St. John's University in September 1963. Being an immature seventeen-year-old for practically my entire freshman year, the school was pretty much party central for me.

In between binges and occasionally hitting the books, I worked as an artists' model. This was at a legitimate art school in Hempstead, Long Island. My job was to look athletic, posing only in a jock strap. That wasn't a stretch at the time.

It was just what I needed: more money for beer.

I also joined the navy reserve. There was no Vietnam War going on at the time, but there was a draft. Back then, it wasn't whether you'd serve, it was with whom. My father was in the French Merchant Marines during World War II.

He was on oil tankers crossing the Atlantic. It was very dangerous to say the least. Some years one thousand ships went down. His father, my grandfather, was on a French Naval ship in Gallipoli where a half million men were killed or wounded in the eight-month battle. The French called it the Battle of the Dardanelles.

My grandfather on my mother's side was on the *USS Arizona* during World War I. He played in the band. The *Arizona* never went overseas when he was on it.

That's why the navy won out over the army and Marine Corps, which was too spit and polish for my misfit tastes.

My six-year commitment included two years active duty. I might have gotten out of the two years if I had stretched out my college enrollment.

This idea was cemented in my mind during boot camp in December 1963 and January 1964 during school break where I froze my balls off in minus-twenty-degree-plus weather at Great Lakes, Illinois.

It was my first trip out of the metro New York area with the exception of a trip to Baltimore when I was in the third grade. It was also my first plane ride.

We took a train from Chicago to Great Lakes. There were thousands of us. DIs shouted, "Line it up, nut to butt. Stay close, nut to butt."

There also were recruits asking, "Anyone from Detroit? Anyone from Charlotte?" And on and on.

I didn't mind getting yelled at by the company commanders and drill instructors. It was the unbelievable stupidity that got me.

The temperature was subfreezing every day we were there. Running on ice caused some to break their legs. Fire drills in the middle of the night where you were standing nude with ice forming on your body would be hazardous to anyone's health. Spit freezes in twenty-four below between the time it leaves your mouth and the time it hits the ground. We tried it to hear its snapping sound.

This was my first exposure to people who couldn't write on more than a second grade level. Some guys sent letters home on the same double-lined paper we used in grade school.

When we mustered out, we were lined up. A so-called doctor with a stethoscope went from one sailor to another saying, "You've got pneumonia, you've got pneumonia," as he made his way down the line. A large number of men were pulled. I was sick as a dog, but it wasn't pneumonia, so I got to go home.

At seventeen, I realized I wasn't suited for anything re-sembling a military career.

A few months later, I found a job at the New York World's Fair. I was a cook at the Missouri Pavilion. I cooked at home but never professionally. I figured only the portions were different. How creative did I have to be? I never said I was a chef.

This was the restaurant part of the pavilion, which sold barbecued beef and ham along with a few other items.

The company was Restaurant Associates. They owned some great restaurants in New York City, including the Four Seasons, the Forum, and the Golden Door at Idlewild which became Kennedy Airport. They also owned a few tourist traps such as Mamma Leone's and the Brass Rail Chain.

Management to its credit realized the help would eventually get sick of eating the same shit they served the customers every day. They bought separate food for the one hundred or so of us who worked there. This included roasts, chops, pastas, and the like.

As I mentioned, I had no experience, but I convinced the person who hired me that I could cook for large numbers of people. It was trial and error. With one exception—I think I did a great job.

I made a birthday cake for one of the workers. I put tons of sugar in Crisco to make the icing. Crisco was just pure white animal fat that looked like icing to me. What did I know? It was the first time I ever saw anyone gag on cake.

Strangely, some people thought it was pretty good.

The company liked me thanks to hard work and a willingness to work long hours at any time of the day or night. I learned to be a short order cook on the overnight shift so we could feed workers at other pavilions.

I became a manager with dozens of people working under me. I was still eighteen.

I took a sabbatical from school. I figured I'd go back after a one semester break. At the end of the summer, almost everyone at the fair was laid off. The company kept me.

Restaurant Associates ran the concession at Wollman's skating rink in Central Park. I worked there as a short order cook. I also worked a hot dog cart in the park.

There was a law on the books at the time that precluded vendors from staying in the same spot for more than a couple of hours. That meant I had to collect everything, including cracker jacks, potato chips, and balloons and move about fifty feet to another site. Then I moved back to the original spot a couple of hours later. Thankfully, that ridiculous law is no longer on the books.

Next, I got a job in the accounts payable department of the American Broadcasting Company. This was across the street from Lincoln Center which was still being built. There were still remnants from the apartment buildings that were replaced. These tenements served as a backdrop for *West Side Story*.

The network's freelance on air talent would send us a bill for their expenses, and we would pay it. My menial job was to put these bills together.

The only notable experience there was constantly being hassled by a then-virtually unknown Howard Cosell who never stopped chasing his money. He was in the office every day complaining to anyone who'd listen about how the company was screwing him.

I was set to go back to school when the navy called me up. I told them I was going back this month, January 1965, but they didn't want to hear it.

The navy gave you a dream sheet when you first got in. You told them where you'd like to be stationed and on what kind of ship. I told them, no aircraft carriers, cruisers, or destroyers. I wanted nothing where you had to be all spit and polish just to pass the time. I didn't see myself as one of those fucking idiots who spent hours shining their shoes and brass belts. I wanted an oiler or freighter. That way I could work in dungarees. I had never been to the West Coast, so I asked to be stationed there.

First, I was sent to a repair ship in Norfolk, Virginia. A few months later, we steamed to Newport, Rhode Island, on a different repair ship. Next was an oil tanker, the *USS*

Neosho.

We went to the Dominican Republic in May and June 1965 during the fighting there. This was another case of us overthrowing an elected government because we didn't like the results. No one remembers this "war" that cost us more than four hundred casualties and more than one thousand Dominican citizens their lives because even historians were too embarrassed to put this on the books.

We sat in Santo Domingo harbor and watched people running from building to building shooting at each other. One time for some unknown reason, we lobbed shells at some targets ashore. A bunch of us were sitting in a room with the chaplain there when the captain kept shouting over the intercom after loud booms from our guns, "Go get 'em boys. We're right on target." He went on during the next ear-splitting volley when I shouted, "Stop it. I'm getting a hard-on."

The place roared. Everyone was laughing. Everyone but the chaplain, that is. He gave me that "you're a lost cause" look and shook his head with disgust.

My main job on the *Neosho* was to sweat out one-hundred-twenty-degree temperatures working in the ship's laundry.

The second you walked in there you were drenched in sweat. The loads of laundry were unending. Then there was the pressing of officers' shirts and pants. I learned to "collar and cuff," which I still did when I ironed my shirts in civilian life. It was a skill I could use to make a living on the "outside" if I happened to be way down and out. The navy promised to teach you skills, but that was ridiculous.

If you had to serve your country, do it as an officer. The

difference between an enlisted man and an officer in the navy was no different than it was between blacks and whites in the South before the Civil Rights Movement. That included separate water fountains, places to eat, shit, and sleep.

On some level, I could see it. We had criminals on board who were given a choice to either join or go to jail. We had people who would have been chronically unemployed if it wasn't for the military. We had real Ku Klux Klan members, not just wannabes. These were some of the vilest racists you'd ever meet.

To call me a misfit was the understatement of the century. I made friends easily. With people in authority, it was another story. I managed to piss off enough of them to get transferred to an ammunition ship, the *USS Mazama* that was bound for Vietnam.

Our job was to transfer millions of pounds of every kind of explosive you can think of except nukes from the Philippines to dozens of points from the Mekong Delta to the Tonkin Gulf off the coast of North Vietnam.

I'd say it sounded worse than it was, but when we were in port, sailors from other ships would buy us drinks because of the real danger they thought we faced.

Because of the volatile nature of our cargo, we weren't allowed to tie into any port. That meant being anchored miles from land when we visited a foreign destination. Our first captain got a letter of complaint from the Governor of Puerto Rico because we tied to a pier in San Juan.

We got shot at, but our man danger was fires. If someone fired on us, we'd make a quick turn and head out to sea. Why not? One unlucky hit, and we were goners. We worked in Vietnam; we didn't fight there.

I remember after being shot at, a number of destroyers appeared out of nowhere and began shelling the beach where the enemy launched rockets at us. I was later ashamed by the elation I felt when I saw the beach being leveled. It was the same elation you feel when your favorite team wins at the final buzzer.

I should mention the confusion while you're getting shot at. Say the people who are shooting at you are three miles away. The incoming rocket or shell is upon you with a whish almost instantly. It takes fifteen seconds for the sound of the enemy's weapons to reach you. So when you hear the *boom* from the shore, you're waiting for shells that already landed. The remedy was to run to general quarters. Your instinct is to run anyway. General quarters gave you a place to run.

I couldn't tell you how many fires there were on that old World War II ship. More than once we heard, "Fire in the ammo hold." Once, we were rearming an aircraft carrier that was alongside when smoke started coming out of our forward ammunition hold. The sailors on the other ship cut our ropes with axes and the carrier fled. That really pissed off our captain who'd have to explain why it happened.

We convinced ourselves if the ship blew up, we'd never know about it.

Once, we delivered magnesium flares to the *USS Oriskany*. Within a couple of hours, one of the flares went off; setting a big fire on the carrier that killed forty-four sailors. It was a horrible tragedy, but many of us were secretly glad those flares were no longer on the *Mazama*.

Our main fear was eating the food that was cooked by guys who kept getting the clap. They weren't allowed to handle the meals once they were diagnosed. Before they made the "clap sheet," who knew?

Some of us suspected they kept getting VD so they wouldn't have to work for two weeks. The cooks were pretty hard edged. One time, one of the guys asked for crunchy peanut butter instead of the smooth stuff they always put out.

"I'll give you crunchy, the next time I take a shit."

You didn't ask a cook, "What's for dinner?"

"How about my balls and spaghetti," or "You want a tube steak?"

None of us were angels. I still have my arrest papers for being locked up in the Philippines for fighting.

I could write a book about all that happened. Every day was something else.

We were lucky to avert a tragedy in Subic Bay, Philippines. We were refueling at an oil depot when a British jet pilot got in trouble, so he bailed out. The jet would have hit the oil tanks which would have been the end of us. Instead, it rammed into a bus in front of the tanks and exploded there. No one was on board the bus except the driver who was burned to death.

We were in the South China Sea when six Chinese gunboats started closing in on us. A cruiser we were rearming leveled its guns at the foreign vessels. They changed course and what could have been a messy incident became a non-event.

We were on our way to Taiwan when we received an SOS from a Lebanese Freighter. The Universal Pride was carrying grain from Red China when it exploded. We rescued three sailors. The very heavy seas tossed the stricken ship like a cork. Water kept rushing over the ship's decks as it list-ed heavily back and forth. Finally, we watched the ship go down. The rest of the crew was lost. Seeing a ship sink is as bad as watching someone die.

We never made it to Taiwan. A sailor on another ammunition ship off Vietnam died from meningitis. The ship was quarantined, so we turned around and went back on line.

I had so many more stories. I can't go through them all.

We went to the Far East through the Panama Canal, stopped in Hawaii, then on to the Philippines. We made an R and R trip to Hong Kong. On the way back to the States, we stopped in Singapore and I hopped over to Malaysia with some shipmates. We went through the Suez Canal and stopped in Beirut, Lebanon.

I was one of only a few who can say he circumnavigated the globe on a ship. I already had a lifetime of adventure. I was only twenty.

Our crew was given a confidential memo when we were almost home. We were ordered to tell people we were never shot at. I'm sure all the hostile action summaries were saved in the situation reports that were sent to the fleet if anyone wanted to look it up. The Pentagon apparently didn't want the public to know how far we were from winning the war. It wasn't long before other ships got hit, ending the illusion that we controlled the coastline.

I read other Pentagon lies in the Stars and Stripes. For instance, the reporters were told we weren't using anti-personnel cluster bomb units in Vietnam. I saw these CBUs with my own eyes. When I think about it, I'm sorry I didn't have the courage to throw them overboard. I could have saved many people a lifetime of heartache.

I knew they were used on women and children as a tool

to demoralize the enemy. They may also have been used on the so-called front lines. I would never do anything to put our guys in jeopardy by tossing them. War was all about contradictions.

All of us had short timer's calendars. It was usually a nude woman. We would color in a numbered body part, and that would let us know how many days we had left to serve.

I had three weeks left when we were crossing the Atlantic on our way to Davisville, Rhode Island, where we were home ported.

For some reason, our commanding officer, Captain Donald Kiley, decided to hold an inspection.

Some of the sailors spent hours shining their shoes so they'd look like patent leather. Their brass buckles would shine as well.

Fuck that.

My shoes were clean and hole free. That was enough for me.

We were lined up on the deck when the captain and some flunky officers walked along the columns of men all sparkling in their uniforms.

When Captain Kiley got to me, he did a double take. "Sailor, those shoes aren't fit for inspection."

I responded briefly, "Twenty-one days, sir."

He shook his head and moved on.

One day, about a dozen or so of us were lounging around in the berthing area when one person asked, who among us will go the farthest when we get back on the "outside."

There were a number of college graduates in the group. Several had great jobs when they got called up. To my surprise, they overwhelmingly said it would be me.

That brought me back to St. John's. When I left it was crew cuts, hootenannies, and the Beach Boys.

When I returned only two years later, it was peace, pot, and pussy. You could also throw in folk-rock, long hair and beards along with the Beatles.

I got involved with radical politics. That included joining SDS, the Young Socialist Alliance, and the Socialist Workers Party. I enjoyed being with anti-war, nonracist, idealistic people. In retrospect, these people never got anywhere because they were more complainers than doers. Grinding out pamphlets and going to demonstrations were good. The hard work was organizing and compromising.

I took part in a demonstration to end the Reserve Officer Training Corps holding classes at St. John's. I didn't think it was a good idea to have young people on a college campus brainwashed by the military.

Unlike every other school in the city, which was predominantly anti-war, St. John's was reactionary conservative.

While we were occupying the ROTC offices, hundreds of pro-war kids demonstrated outside alumni hall where ROTC was housed.

So here were about fifty anti-war demonstrators, some afraid for their lives, wondering how this would end.

At first, the protesters sang Lennon's "Give Peace a Chance," which was on the charts at the time along with Donovan's "Atlantis" and other peace anthems.

Then it started getting late and the angry crowd outside grew larger and more wild-eyed.

"Let's call the cops," one thin, long-haired young man blurted out.

I stood up. "Are you shitting me? The cops will beat the shit out of you before these kids outside will. How do you think a nightstick would feel up your ass?"

A girl with metal rimmed glasses sobbed, "I have to get to class. I can't miss it. What can I do?"

I told her to come with me.

We walked outside and through the screaming hoard. I might get my lumps, but I'd make it worth my while.

The crowd opened like the Red Sea.

No one bothered us. I didn't take into account that I was fairly well-known on campus as the veteran who tended bar across the street.

I got involved with teaching adults to get their GEDs, and I worked with kids at a South Jamaica elementary school so they could have a slightly better chance against their counterparts in the suburbs.

It was usually husbands and wives who came to the GED sessions. In every instance, the wife was smarter than the husband. Eventually a husband would drop out. Then the woman who was a shoo-in to get her diploma also dropped out because of pressure at home.

South Jamaica was so rough at the time that the priest who ran the program when I was there was forced to beg for his life on his knees before he was murdered by two men.

I boxed at the Upper Park Avenue Community Center on 125th Street in Harlem to stay in shape and to release some of the anger I had for no real reason.

It was a great education for me. I didn't like all the skipping rope and running, but you can't cheat; otherwise you'd be sucking air hard after about a minute in the ring.

I was a pretty decent fighter. The trainers were older, formerly successful boxers. They gave their time for free.

One of them fought hall of fame champions Sandy Sadler and Willie Pep. We'd see him leave his shoe shine box in the locker room before he came out to help us.

Sometimes he was homeless.

"I'd get myself arrested for vagrancy in the winter. That way I'd get a warm place to stay at Rikers Island. The city shelters are the pits."

"I can't believe the shelters were worse."

"Yeah, with all the thieves rolling people who are sleeping. Sometimes from Rikers we'd take a boat ride to Hart Island where the city has its potters' field. The new graves are situated on top of the old ones. The bodies and the boxes they were in deteriorate in about seven years. There are hundreds of thousands of people buried in a small area. Once in a while, we'd see a skull and we'd play soccer with it."

He was pretty articulate. One of the professional fighters in the gym was badly brain-damaged. Every state has a boxing commission. New York's was pretty strict. You would have to wait at least one month, maybe more, before fighting again if you were knocked out. You could take a fight in another state that was lax. I remember he came in a week after being KO'd and was offered a bout the next day in Maine.

"I'll take anything," he said in a Crazy Guggenheim sort of way.

Seeing all this put a damper on any chance I'd have at a boxing career. I started to notice my head ached every time I took a punch. I wore headgear, but that was used mainly to prevent cuts. Originally, you tune out any pain and just work. I started to wonder whether I'd eventually get punchy. When you start to notice your head aching, you have no chance. Real fighters don't care.

I joined the Veterans' Club at St John's. It was like a fraternity. The group consisted mainly of pro-war conservatives. There were some real war heroes at the school. One got the Navy Cross for calling air strikes on his own position. We had Silver Star and Bronze Star winners. We had many wounded vets who were still recovering. Some were amputees. One marine was blinded in action. We had guys who served on submarines. We had several Green Berets along with combat infantrymen and paratroopers. Some served in remote bases in Korea, West Germany, and even Alaska. One of our members died of leukemia due to his exposure to Agent Orange.

We had cops and firefighters who joined after serving in the military. One of our members had a job working high construction.

"If you fall from the third floor or the thirtieth, it's all the same. You don't think about it."

Pro and anti-war lines were drawn between us. This was the late 1960s.

Some of our arguments were loud enough to attract the attention of everyone in the cafeteria. We drew crowds of onlookers.

We convinced the school to let us have our own freshman orientation. I had a beard and long hair and the new students still had military haircuts.

I told them, "In six months, you'll look like me."

I remember in Vietnam, it was all, "This sucks." "What are we doing here, anyway?" "Fuck the lifers." "Fuck the officers." Some officers were afraid to go on deck at night, lest they disappear into the South China Sea.

Now the attitude was "fuck these kids. If I had to go, they should."

Another mantra was "we have to fight communism. Better there than here."

The bottom line was we were all veterans. We had a right to disagree, and disagree we did.

We didn't always argue. We took classes together. We shared books. We met each other's families. We got into barroom brawls against strangers and had each other's backs.

There was nothing like singing along to tunes like the Clancy Brothers' "Rising of the Moon" or Janis Joplin's "Piece of My Heart," which were on the jukebox at the pub across the street from the school.

Most of these vets were the greatest guys I'd ever met. They were funny. They were great storytellers. They were generous. I loved them.

Somehow, they elected me their president.

I couldn't rely on the GI bill to pay for school. That came to one hundred bucks a month, which was "generously" upped to one hundred thirty by the time I graduated. That was beer money.

I worked a couple of summers as an overnight guard in the New York Stock Exchange. That's where I had my first encounter with ghosts.

When we walked our post, there was always someone who seemed to be working under a dim light in one of the basement offices. I asked the elevator operator who had been at the exchange for almost fifty years who it was.

"Oh, that's so and so (I can't remember the name). He jumped during the crash of '29. Everybody sees him there."

Needless to say, every guard ran past that office when they were walking their posts.

We made it worse on ourselves by hiding in parts of the darkened building so we could scare any guard who happened to be walking by. We acted like kids, even though our group consisted of ex-cops, Vietnam vets, and even one guy, an ex-cop, who lied about his age to join the marines after Pearl Harbor and ended up spending his seventeenth birthday fighting on Guadalcanal.

I had other jobs. I was a chauffeur for Fugazy Limousine Service.

On my first day on the job, the dispatcher assigned a driver to show me the ropes. John Cavallo was to retire after his shift was over. The dispatcher changed his mind and sent Cavallo to the airport in an old nine seat limo. He gave me another teacher.

Cavallo's limo ran out of gas on the Van Wyck Expressway. He was killed when a car ran into him as he poured fuel in the tank from a can. I shudder to think that could have been me. I never would have let the elderly man fill the car himself.

Besides private jobs, we had a contract with a few airlines to take pilots and stewardesses to and from the airports and the hotels in New York City. More often than not, it seemed the pilots were drunk when they got into my car after a flight.

I hit a car while parking at the TWA terminal at Kennedy airport. There was no one in the vehicle, and mine wasn't damaged. I had seen this ploy before, so I tried it. I wrote on a paper, "People are watching me. They think I'm giving you my license plate and phone number. I'm not. Sorry about that."

I put the note on the windshield and drove away.

I got a summer job with International Teletype and Telegraph. I was to "service" companies that had telex machines, which were used instead of telephones to communicate between businesses overseas. The man who took me around told me it was really a sales job. He was a Willy Loman type. I could see in the eyes of the customers they wanted nothing to do with him. I couldn't live with a job where people tried to avoid me.

I gave ITT notice when we got back after day one. I told them there was no way could I do sales. To their great credit, they paid me for two weeks' work.

I also drove a cab and tended bar in a couple of places just off campus.

I didn't know my way around the city very well and I didn't know how to mix drinks either.

I already had a chauffeur's license. The test to get my hack license was ridiculously easy. You were given a paper with ten locations on it. I was given a week to study it. You were required to name only seven locations in order to pass. Remarkably, some would be drivers failed.

As far as tending bar, there were mostly students who drank mainly beer. If someone wanted an off-the-wall mixed drink, I would look it up in a book I bought for the occasion.

St. John's didn't have dorms. About six of us rented a house in Maspeth just off the Long Island Expressway. I wrote about six because dozens of Veterans' Club members stayed there at one time or another.

The goings on there will have to remain classified.

Sometimes, those of us who drove cabs would arrange to meet at McCann's on 48th and Lexington Avenue in Manhattan just to shoot the shit. Of course, if you were stuck in the Bronx or somewhere else, you couldn't make it.

At McCann's, you could get a three-inch thick corned beef on rye and a beer for a dollar. It was a great place to talk and laugh and feel good about ourselves.

I worked as a bartender in two different places. At the time, I drank too much for my own good. This would help me kill two birds with one stone.

I got paid, and I never drank while working. That was a hard-and-fast rule for me.

My father and his brother, my uncle Francois, had owned a bar in the Bronx in the late '50s and early '60s. The majority of these places in New York City were what we'd call "deege" bars, short for degenerate. Others called them dive bars. Most bars in the city were dive bars back in the day. I didn't want to turn out like the barflies who practically had stools named after them.

I learned as I went along. I was generous with buy backs. I took care of my friends. I was light on the liquor for the female drinkers. Only one wasn't happy.

"Hey, Bob, how about putting some balls in this drink."

I had to keep the peace. I wasn't very intimidating at around one hundred fifty pounds. One evening after a classic barroom brawl, one of the customers asked, "Do you expect trouble tonight?"

"No, I don't think so. Why?"

"Because they same guys who started last night's fight are here again, and they brought some friends."

I called them over and told them, "We need to have a quiet night tonight. How about a round of drinks on the house."

They were agreeable. They drank up and left.

This took me to January 1970 and graduation. My brother, Elliott, was also scheduled to graduate at the same time.

St. John's was reactionary enough to bring in Kate Smith as the main graduation speaker. She was known for two things: her girth and her rendition of "God Bless America," which the pro war types hi-jacked into making it one of their anthems.

My brother and I boycotted the ceremony. I'm sad about that now. We were the first in our family to graduate college. It would have been a treat for our parents who deserved to be there. I remembered this every time St John's tried to hit me up for money.

At this point, I thought I needed a straight job.

My degree in marketing got me an interview at the Royal Globe Insurance Company. They sold me on this great training program that set the standard in the industry. This also included a halfway decent and steady pay check.

I'd be a commercial insurance underwriter. No sales were involved. It sounded interesting enough to consider. You'd make your company take millions and millions of dollars in risks after evaluating safety and other likelihoods of loss.

On the other hand, something in the back of my mind told me insurance might be the last thing I wanted to do. Maybe I took the job to shut my friends up.

Here I was, a twenty-four-year-old college graduate still alternately driving a cab and tending bar.

I was single and having a good time. I knew it couldn't last forever. I took the job. It would do until the real thing came along.

Years later, I realized I didn't want the world to pass me by. I had to somehow change careers—but to what?

I had no special talents that I knew of. Accounting is boring. I couldn't open a store. What would I sell, anyway? Eventually, I would hate it. What about teaching? Forget it. Teach what?

Then I heard an ad on the radio pushing a broadcasting school.

Forty-seven

It's the Same Old Song

August 1, 1981

The two hours digging the trench made me realize it was time for me to make another last ditch effort, no pun intended, to get a real-paying job in the business.

This time I'd try something offbeat since nothing else worked.

Here's what I sent out with a self-addressed, stamped envelope:

PLEASE RETURN IN THE ENCLOSED ENVELOPE

___ I may have an immediate on/off air position for you. Please call me at once.

___You'd be a real asset to my newsroom, but my budget is leaner than yours.

___However, I may have a position opening soon.

___However, I could use someone to freelance in your area. Let's talk.

___I'll keep your resume on file.

___If you really have your heart set on working in New York City, I suggest you buy a cart and sell warm pretzels.

Here was hoping.

A few world and national stories kicked off the first weekend in August.

One biggie was the MTV launch. Its promise was spelled out in its first song, "Video Killed the Radio Star."

It looked good. The problem is you can listen to a song hundreds of times. Can you watch the same video that many times? Can you watch it three times? Can you watch it in your car?

I didn't think we'd be obsolete anytime soon.

Anything could happen. My grandfather was a musician. One of his jobs was to play his horn in the pit during the silent movie era. Music didn't come with the films. Once talkies came out, he had to find another job, so he joined a band. Who would have guessed?

Another top story was the strike by air traffic controllers. Hundreds of flights were threatened.

A seventh and eighth hunger striker died in the Maze Prison. There was some rioting, but nothing like what happened five months ago when Bobby Sands died.

Closer to home, the town of Ramapo found a way to legalize illegal homes in ultra orthodox Jewish and Hasidic sections of Monsey.

The town also relaxed zoning to permit large developments already in the works to double in size. This would open the floodgates for tens of thousands of people from overcrowded parts of Brooklyn to come up here.

August 3, 1981

Leaders at Stewart Airport tried to find ways to handle international flights that would have flown into JFK and Newark Airports.

Stewart's air traffic controllers weren't members of the striking union, commonly known as PATCO. Frank Tarbell was general manager of the airport in Newburgh.

"We have no way of knowing whether flights will be diverted here. If they do, we're prepared for them. We have a twelve-thousand-foot runway, we're fully instrumented and we can handle traffic in category two weather. That makes us one of the most modern facilities anywhere."

August 4, 1981

Belton Brims headed back to Rockland for trial. He decided to waive extradition.

An assistant DA from Alabama told us off tape that Selma has law enforcement people who know how to deal with belligerent suspects.

"Let's just say they had a 'discussion,' and Brims decided he didn't like it here. We'll try him on the robbery charges after his case is taken care of up north. Brims is a predicate felon so he'd get life in prison if he's convicted of any charge in Alabama."

President Reagan promised to fire striking air traffic controllers if they didn't get back on the job.

August 5, 1981

We called Sheriff Lindemann on Brims.

"I'm sending my best men to pick him up. They know what they're doing. That guy is going to be taken care of in jail like any other prisoner. If they listened to me before, none of this would have happened."

"Can you give us any details?"

"We have six drivers going down in two cars. The ride has nothing to do with the air controllers' strike. I just don't want Brims on a plane."

Rockland's three veterans' cemeteries were finally put into better shape. Who knew how long that would last. County lawmakers balked at hiring any full-timers to care for the grounds. They opted for either hiring seasonal help or an outside contractor to do the job.

I hope someone remembers this come election time when they come begging at American Legion and VFW halls. I have my doubts. For some reason, veterans are the biggest dupes when it comes to voting for their own interests. Let me go on record here with a message for brain dead vets who see themselves as shitheads or useless peons.

Wake the fuck up!

August 6, 1981

Ken Gribetz was back lobbying for a single trial in the Sohn case. "We will not have to put the witnesses through the hardship of having to testify on two occasions. In addition, each trial would take a lengthy period of time. It would not be fair to the criminal justice system to have to go through this procedure on two occasions."

Long gone were the days when the working man showed solidarity with unions. Already, thousands lined up to replace striking air traffic controllers.

The government printed tens of thousands of fliers describing what it took to qualify. A new day has dawned for organized labor.

Speaking of strikes, Major League Baseball came up with a plan for how the remainder of the season will play out.

Would you believe a split season?

Teams in first place in their respective divisions when the strike began would play the winners of the second half. After that, the playoffs and World Series would remain the same.

August 8, 1981

I usually made my own breakfast, but Eti and I were going to my brother's birthday party later, so I got lazy.

A deli near us had this sign, "Bacon, cheese, and egg on a roll for $.50."

This was a stretch for me because I was a vegetarian for several years. Bacon is probably the worst meat you can eat.

Anyway, the price was right. I ordered two, one for Eti and the other for me.

"That's a dollar thirty."

I looked at the sign, and it still said fifty cents each. I pointed it out to the counterman.

"The sign says it should be a dollar."

"Do you believe everything you read?"

"Not really." I handed him the dollar thirty.

Before we left, I noticed a tip cup on the counter.

"You want a tip? How about the tip of my joint?"

No, you can't believe everything you read. This reminded me of when I bartended at a pub across the street from St. John's University while I was going there. The drinking age was eighteen, so the local bars were generally packed with college kids, especially at night.

The pub was licensed to serve beer only.

Behind the bar were eight faux kegs with spigots and tap handles with names that included Ballantine Ale, Ballantine Beer, Piels, Rheingold, Schaeffer, Budweiser, Schlitz, and Pabst. I loved the ale. Back then, it had a bitter woodsy taste. The other beers seemed a bit sour. That may have been the result of the pipes rarely being cleaned.

The Ballantine beer never sold. The kids universally said it tasted like piss. The claimed they wouldn't drink it, even if it was free.

It was always, "I can't drink anything but Schaefer." Or "I've never had better beer than Rheingold."

They couldn't know the pub owner had a deal with Ballantine. All the pipes from Piels, Rheingold, Schaeffer, Budweiser, Schlitz, and Pabst led to Ballantine kegs in the basement.

Everyone drank Ballantine. No, you couldn't believe everything you read, not even beer tap handles.

Belton Brims was back at the Rockland County jail.

Sheriff's Patrol Chief James Kralik was one of the six who made the twenty-five-hundred-mile round trip.

"Brims behaved himself. We basically had two officers assigned to him who would be normally responsible for bringing him back. The remaining officers were responsible for the continuous driving of the van. Brims was in an extremely good mood when he got here."

Sheriff Ray Lindemann said security around Brims was to remain very tight.

"He'll be in a cell by himself with a deputy on him 'round the clock. It's twenty-four hours a day with a corrections officer around him all the time."

He forgot about security when he paraded Brims, who was chained like a circus animal, in front of the news media.

Why not, it was a circus atmosphere.

I was standing between Evan Weiner and Fran Schneidau with cameras all around. Brims got to within two feet of us.

He gave us a scary savage look and kept walking.

Forty-eight

A Legendary Visit

August 10, 1981

I had just finished my eight o'clock cast when a middle-aged man who looked like a typical WRKL listener walked into the newsroom.

You know by now what I mean, a rural look consisting of a clean flannel shirt and pants worn a bit high around the waist.

"I was driving by and thought I'd stop in. I helped your old owner, Al Spiro, set up the equipment here. I knew him when he was a chief engineer at WNEW years ago. I bet you still have the ITA board in the main studio and the Sparta in the production area.

"I'm Les Paul."

Wow, I was in the presence of a legend. No one ever told me he set this place up.

I told him, "We still play your stuff. I love 'Vaya Con Dios' and 'How High the Moon.' In fact, I have your greatest hits album with Mary Ford in my collection at home."

He looked pleased.

"I'm over in Mahwah. I know you. I'm a regular listener."

We chatted a bit about the equipment which was a bit technical for me when "Jet Airliner" by the Steve Miller Band came through the speakers. It might have been a cosmic event.

Les Paul looked toward the air studio, "That's Steve Miller. I gave him his first guitar lesson when he was about five. His parents were best man and maid of honor at my wedding. That was 1949 in Wisconsin."

He walked around the main office for a couple of minutes and stopped to talk with Carl Nathe. Then he returned to the newsroom.

"I better go. It was nice meeting you."

We shook hands and he left.

August 11, 1981

Carl Nathe said he was still pissed off at Bob Marvin for an embarrassing incident that happened last year.

"I convinced him to let me cover the Westchester Open Golf Tournament. Something like that is easy to get sponsored. I should have known he can't even sell loose joints at a 'Legalize It' demonstration. Unfortunately for me, the only thing the sales people could come up with was a trade with Budget Rent-a-Truck."

My first thought was Marvin is going to shit when he

finds out I'm still driving the rented Budget Pontiac around.

"What's so bad about that?" I asked.

"It would have been okay, except Budget insisted we take one of their trucks to the tournament so people could see their logo. Maybe one of the sales people could have driven it, but no. I got elected. I had to sit low in the truck and hide my face every time I saw someone I recognized. That's how embarrassed I was. What's worse, after the tournament, a writer from the *Journal News* offered to give me a lift to my car. I let him drop me off next to someone else's. I pretended to put the key in the door while the writer drove off. Then I crawled back to the truck. I'll think twice before I ask Marvin to come up with a sponsor for something. What a loser."

Pretty soon, my sister-in-law would be making as little as those of us in the newsroom.

Pan American asked its workers to take another 10 percent pay cut. The carrier also asked its unions to freeze wages after the cut until the end of next year.

The obviously mismanaged company lost more than two hundred million dollars in the first six months of this year. That was up from losses of about one hundred forty million from the same time last year.

August 12, 1981

Bob Marvin was "overheard" over the phone bashing one of our reporters.

It was to someone from United Way who wanted to give that person an award. We couldn't figure out who it was since we all cover fluff events that end with the radio station getting another plaque to hang on the wall.

"No, I wouldn't do anything for him. He's really mediocre. He's lazy. To be honest, he's only working here because we feel sorry for him."

Thanks for the loyalty, scumbag. This prick treated all of us like shit.

August 14, 1981

Belton Brims was back in court, and this time it was no more mister nice guy. He showed up handcuffed and shackled with a chain around his waist.

Everything was okay until Judge Isaac Rubin relieved Conrad Lynn as Brims' lawyer and replaced him with Bennett Gershman.

Gershman was not a Rocklander. He was a Pace University Law School professor. It wasn't long before trouble began. Brims told Gershman that he wanted civil rights lawyer C. Vernon Mason to assist in his defense.

Judge Rubin told Brims Mason is handling another case, adding Gershman was adequate. That's when Brims exploded.

"Fuck this. It's not your life that's on the fucking line. I should be able to pick my own fucking lawyer."

This went on for about two minutes before Rubin ordered him back to his cell.

"You don't intimidate me."

However, Gershman was visibly shaken as Brims was led in chains to his cell by six guards who had surrounded him during the angry outburst.

Conrad Lynn was in the courtroom while all this was

going on. "I wanted to take a little vacation later on this fall and now I may be able to do it," he squealed happily.

August 16, 1981

Carl Nathe and I broke our asses tonight to get the stuff for the morning news out. That meant we could head out to the Mount Ivy Pub for a couple of drinks before last call.

Rich Mendelson was watching the fort. I saw him in the back scrounging around for some blank tapes.

He was apparently working on his air checks so he didn't need us snooping around. He tried as hard as everyone else to get out of here.

Carl told me something good should be happening soon. Here's hoping.

I broke down and returned the Pontiac Rent-a-Car. I bought a 1971 Capri which I named the blue bullet. It ran, it was clean, and it had an AM-FM radio. Sweet. I wasn't high maintenance.

August 17, 1981

Eti and I took our preliminary wedding pictures at "the castle" across the river in Westchester. This was so we weren't too hassled during the actual event.

It would be a royal pain in the ass to be interrupted all night by an enterprising photographer who was only trying to do his job. This should help.

Of course, Eti looked great in her wedding dress. She got it for fifty dollars because she modeled it at a Calvin

Klein event.

I wore a gray suit. I'd be wearing a tux for the wedding. Maybe no one will notice when they look at the album.

I hope Eti didn't notice there was a cross on one of the parapets. Maybe it was Jews for Jesus.

Forty-nine

Motel Picket Line

August 18, 1981

There had been union talk going on for a while here. Bringing one in would surely get Bob Marvin fired.

Some were all for it, others were happy as pigs in shit making a big two hundred bucks a week. A representative from NABET came by.

He realized the problem the radio station faced. There was only so much money in the pot. It wasn't like our sales people were driving Bentleys around.

I drove the rental Pontiac for months, so I didn't want to be too ungrateful.

On the other hand, Marvin's disloyalty to his news team along with me digging a cesspool trench were grating to say the least.

Luckily, I had to work, so there would be no job action

for me. The union rep pushed job security—bullshit like if you were let go it could only be for cause. In real life, they can't do more than take your money.

Freelancers Tony Winton and Tobin Coleman were the most militant. Both did high-quality work for us.

Winton went to Columbia J-school. He could write his own ticket. Despite that, he cared more about his co-workers than he did his career. We learned by tapping into the phone that Bob Marvin and Barrie would be at the Rockland Motel on Route 202 in the afternoon.

Bob and Barrie went through their usual routine, which was funny because everyone knew what was going on. They would leave the station separately and a few minutes apart.

They would return a couple of hours later, also separately and a few minutes apart.

A few staffers, including Steve Possell who finally saw the light, picketed in front of the motel with signs that read, "Only one man gets the big raise at WRKL," "Beat it," and "WRKL is 'hard on' its workers."

They weren't on motel property, but the manager nicely asked them to leave, so they did.

August 19, 1981

Marvin was really outraged by yesterday's demonstration. I guess the motel manager told him about it. Our phone tapping informants said he went through dozens of tapes and resumes and called to see if anyone was still interested.

I told Evan Weiner I got a job covering the action in El Salvador.

"Are you taking Eti with you?"

"Of course I am. We'd make a dynamic news combination there. What do you think?"

"Well, it's safer than New York. I got my pocket picked the other day while I was in the elevator at Madison Square Garden.

"Lucky I'm a newsman. They only got three dollars."

Then, he started complaining about his love life.

"Being twenty-five is a bad age because older girls want men twenty years older than them and what can you talk about with a twenty or twenty-one-year old?"

"I don't know, Evan. You can always figure out something to say."

August 20, 1981

President Reagan brought America's bully image back. Jimmy Carter was the only president in U.S. history to have none of our servicemen killed in action during his term in office.

That was apparently too wimpy for Reagan's tastes. His idea was to go after a weak nation that couldn't hurt us. Libya was at the top of his list.

Moammar Gadaffy was on the unapproved dictator roster.

This was the same Reagan who trashed Israel for taking out Iraq's nuclear program.

Yesterday, he ordered two navy fighter jets to shoot down two Libyan fighters after what the Pentagon called an unprovoked attack.

This happened off the Gulf of Sidra. Libya said the gulf

is theirs. Reagan said it was international. He said he ordered the maneuvers to show, in his words, "America has the muscle to back up its words."

The White House released a photo of Reagan "taking the helm of the carrier *USS Constellation*," wearing a jacket and hat with the ship's logo embossed.

I bet it felt like he was on the back lot again, where he saw all his combat during World War II.

August 23, 1981

It was a busy night here for tourists.

First, Barrie Lipscomb came around with one of her numerous boyfriends. They were on their way to go dancing and happened to stop by. Barrie took the guy into the production studio. She had the presence of mind to bring in a few carts with commercials on them. I guessed she thought we didn't know what was going on.

I never saw her so made up, not that there was any improvement.

Later, she came up to me. She mentioned a news woman who worked here before my time. She had the balls to say the woman was our age.

I should have told her in front of her boyfriend, "Barrie, you're at least ten years older than me. Who are you bullshitting?"

Barrie had no problem putting it to me. "Her father was ancient and married someone twenty years younger."

I sensed a dig in there somewhere. She left and in walked Dave Peters with a girl.

He must have listened to the Rich Mendelson lecture

on how a tour of the radio station will get you an automatic roll in the hay with even the most virtuous, resistant young ladies.

Peters really worked overtime showing this one around. He went through how a newscast is put together.

"This is local radio, so we always lead with top local stories. If it's national, we try to localize it. We don't block the news, but we put stories together that make sense. If there's a local housing controversy, we'll put it together with the national housing crisis, and so forth."

Then he showed her how the carts work and how to check the wire machine. He even called New Jersey Governor Brendan Byrne's line to show her how the news is taken in over the phone.

Tomorrow, he's going to tell me he's engaged.

I grabbed a couple of rolls of toilet paper and went home.

August 24, 1981

I was alone in the newsroom when Barrie walked in.

"I know many of the people here don't think much of me. I have a husband who spends practically every waking minute trying to make as much money as he can. That's how it is."

"Don't worry about what people think. They like you a lot more than you realize."

Mark David Chapman got less than he deserved. He was sentenced today to twenty years to life for killing John Lennon.

The former mental patient wouldn't go for the insanity

defense his lawyer recommended. He pleaded guilty in June to killing Lennon.

Wearing a bulletproof vest, Chapman read a passage from *Catcher in the Rye*, saying the book explained his reason for killing the ex-Beatle. Before the sentencing, a defense psychiatrist said Chapman was a paranoid schizophrenic who had experienced delusions since childhood.

Chapman was taken to Sing Sing prison in Westchester.

A fight that began in Trinidad three and a half years ago ended yesterday with a fatal shooting.

Neil John of Brooklyn was accused of gunning down Michael Chacon at the Anthony Wayne parking lot.

DA Kenneth Gribetz said Chacon was coincidently from Brooklyn, but the two hadn't seen each other since their days on the Caribbean island.

"During the course of the incident three years ago, John was slashed across his face by Chacon which caused a six-inch scar. "Every time John looked at his disfigurement in the mirror, he saw Chacon. When Chacon saw John yesterday in the state park's picnic area, he kept telling people, 'This is my last day on earth. This is my last day on earth.'"

"This was the first time since the fight that they had seen each other. John later went up to the victim and proceeded to fire six shots at him."

After the shooting, John escaped into the woods. He was captured by park police without a struggle nine and a half hours later when he was spotted leaving the area by car.

Police were still looking for the small caliber pistol used in the crime.

August 25, 1981

One man died and a passenger was in critical condition after their car went out of control and landed in Lake De-Forest.

The fast-moving car took out eighty feet of guardrail and a chain link fence along Congers Road.

Clarkstown Police diver Bill Garbus told reporter Rich Komonchak that officers were already at the scene when he arrived.

"I was instructed to put my dive gear on and start searching for the person who was in the car. I found him about five feet from the vehicle in about five feet of water. The car was on its roof, and you could see the four tires sticking out. The lake wasn't deep, but visibility was about five inches. There were several civilians in the water who had removed the other victim."

A Clarkstown officer said the speed limit on the causeway was only thirty miles an hour.

"Witnesses say the car was moving in excess of sixty miles an hour. At that speed, the inverted type rail we have almost acts like a launching ramp. The vehicle hits it, mounts it, and it puts it in a trajectory if it's going fast enough to the hurricane fence. So the car was launched into the water."

More than four hundred outraged and angry homeowners converged on Ramapo Town Hall to fight a proposed down zoning that would downgrade the nature of their neighborhoods and destroy their property values.

The new zone would permit semi-attached two family homes in a one family home area.

The change would be to accommodate the lifestyles preferred by Hasidic Jews who were flocking into the community.

There were already hundreds of illegally converted homes throughout the town. Some of the one family homes housed four and five rather large families.

Town Board candidate Debra Chiatt said violations were not enforced. "This is a rubber stamp board that's concerned with getting reelected."

Supervisor Mort Baron told the belligerent audience he couldn't ignore nine hundred signatures on a petition brought to him by Hasidic leaders.

A Hasidic speaker told the board, "You are forcing us to violate laws."

A resident shouted to him, "If you can't afford to live single family, you have no right to be here. If I can't pay my mortgage, the bank kicks me out."

Another said, "You're an invading army with your own laws. Rabbis tell their congregation who to vote for. No one dares dissent. It's outrageous that women aren't allowed to vote in the same booths as the men. This is supposed to be America."

After four hours, the board voted to approve the zone change and to pave the way for a new 112-unit development nearby.

August 26, 1981

Medical Examiner Dr. Frederick Zugibe finished his autopsy on shooting victim Michael Chacon.

"Chacon was hit from behind by three thirty-two-caliber bullets. One of the bullets hit the victim's skull. It didn't penetrate it. Another lodged in Chacon's buttock. The bullet that killed Chacon entered his back just below one of his kidneys."

Neil John was held on seventy five thousand dollars bail pending a grand jury hearing.

Linda Winikow was in a talkative mood. I don't know how long she went on without coming up for air. When she finally paused, I told her I didn't understand what she said.

"Could you start over?"

She believed me and, for a change, was at a loss for words. After I told her I was kidding, she went on for another ten minutes.

Barrie Lipscomb was talking on the phone in the rear of the newsroom.

"My husband is coming back from a business trip. He wants to take me to a show and dinner. I guess I'll have to reward him with sex."

Fifty

Now Pitching, Sandy Baron

August 27, 1981

Sandy Baron, the comedian, called the newsroom. Tim Scheld gave the phone to me. Baron started by offering to buy me a drink.

"I've been listening to radio stations in the metro area, and I think I can do something really special for you guys. Can we get together?"

"OK," I told him. "The station signs off at seven thirty. I can meet you somewhere in the county sometime after that. I'll bring another reporter with me."

"There's a lounge in the Holiday Inn on Route 303 in Orangeburg. I'll be there."

I had one more newscast before I went off the air.

The theme from "Deliverance" was playing over the speakers. This was my signal that I had to hurry. As I mentioned before, instrumentals led into the newscasts. I always waited until the last minute, in case there was another good story to tell.

I gathered my scripts and grabbed a couple of carts.

I raced through the small production studio and gave the carts to the DJ.

I was all set.

After I was done, I told Carl Nathe we were leaving for a couple of hours and asked him to handle the phones for us.

Tim and I got there at around eight thirty.

Baron had a down-and-out look when we spotted him at the bar. I hate to say seedy.

He looked like he could use a meal. I wondered if he'd be insulted if I told him about the government's free cheese program.

I thought of him as a Borscht Belt comic although I remembered he was on the Johnny Carson show numerous times and he co-hosted a show with Della Reese in the late '60s.

He was drinking beer and smoking. Tim and I ordered Budweisers.

We talked for a couple of minutes before I came up with one of my usual faux pas.

"I remember you doing some 'Love Boat' episodes."

"No, I'm probably the only actor in Hollywood who didn't do that show. Maybe you're thinking about the movie *If It's Tuesday, This Must Be Belgium*."

"Maybe that's it."

Tim said, "He's probably thinking about *Love American Style*."

I didn't say anything. Both those shows were shit as far

331

as I was concerned.

"I know you wrote 'Natural Man' that Lou Rawls sang."
I asked, "Was it autobiographical?"

"Sort of. I wrote it with Bobby Hebb who wrote 'Sunny.'
Lou Rawls really sold it. 'Lenny' was somewhat biographical.
I did the shows in Los Angeles and on Broadway. I should
have done the movie. Dustin was great, but there's a soul to
standup that Lenny and I shared that would have come out."

Then Baron said, "I have a great idea for a morning show.
I'll host. I'll bring in name guests. Many of them live nearby.
We're close to New York City, so that wouldn't be a problem.
I do improv. I think people would rather listen to comedy in
the morning and interesting personalities than news about
kids getting ready for school. They get ready for school this
time every year. My show will bring in big ratings. Big ratings mean big commercial dollars."

My personal belief was that a show like that would be
kick-ass, especially in New York City.

I knew Bob Marvin's reaction already. I mentioned them.

"Two things: why would he pay someone good money when he can get one of us for squat? We get paid shit.
Most important, local news is our bread and butter. There's
no way you can have a heavy load of news in the afternoon
with virtually none in the morning. I'm positive there's plenty of room for funny morning shows with guests, but this
is a tough sell, especially to a general manager who can't sell
Thunderbird to a wino.

"I'll try."

"If the show is good, you'll laugh and if the show is shit,
you'll laugh."

We were there for another half hour or so. Baron told us

a few stories about some of the stars he worked with.

I told him his morning show sounded like a great idea. Then Tim and I left.

August 28, 1981

Sandy Baron would have had a better chance if he did local sports. That's because Carl Nathe just gave notice.

He's going to a Casper, Wyoming, television station where he'll anchor sportscasts and do Wyoming University football and basketball play by play.

He said he'd stick around for about three weeks until Marvin found a replacement.

Good for him!

Meanwhile, Bob Marvin said no to a Sandy Baron morning show. "You know, if he developed a big audience, he'd leave. Then what would we have? Our loyal listeners would be gone, and we'd have to start from scratch."

I let Tim call Baron with the news.

Carl, Tim Scheld, Steve Roy, and a couple of others went next door to "Our Gang" for what turned out to be a night of free drinks.

Tim was a Pac-Man wizard. He took on all comers for booze, and he never lost. We all got very shitfaced.

He said you can't succeed at anything without a great will to win. That was the secret. *True*. You needed a great will. That would go hand in hand in this business with a great curiosity and an ethic that caused you to work incredible hours because you couldn't bring yourself to do it any other way.

You also should be a Yenta who just has to be the first to tell someone the story.

Fifty-one

They Let Him Out

August 29, 1981

Ben Gershman apparently won over Belton Brims.

He said some of the evidence against Brims was taken illegally, that his civil rights may have been violated. He also moved for a change of venue because of what he called undue publicity.

I asked him about the escape.

"Brims didn't escape."

"What do you mean? He wasn't in the lockup. He was in Alabama."

"He didn't escape, the jailers let him out. That's his defense."

"I don't get it."

"It all came out in the grand jury investigation."

Gershman looked serious.

"The corrections officers heard sawing for several days. The day before Brims left, a guard ran into him on the fourth tier. In fact, Brims went up to him and shouted 'boo'. The officer ran out of there."

I snickered, "You're kidding."

Gershman went on. "The skylight was left open to let fresh air in. That's how he left. They're all afraid of Lindemann, so no one said anything. No one even wrote a report on an inmate walking free. I'm telling you, they let Brims go. They practically told him to leave."

August 30, 1981

Dave Peters must be getting serious about his new girlfriend. He started complaining about the money he's making. He wrote a new song he wanted to get published, and he's calling his squeeze all the time now.

"I'm telling Rich Mendelson I don't want to go to too many meetings at night anymore."

August 31, 1981

Bob Marvin already found Carl Nathe's replacement. Barry Sachs was a young man from Spring Valley. Welcome to the world of minimum wage rock and roll, Barry.

In Spring Valley, cheating on your girlfriend could be deadly.

I spoke to several witnesses who gave me the whole story about our latest local homicide. They said Annette Whitlock and Ernie George had been fighting for weeks.

"I heard Annette screaming at Ernie, 'Don't ever do to me what you did last night.'"

"Then Ernie walked out of his apartment and onto the driveway with a knife in his chest. I asked him if he was okay."

"No, she done killed me."

I walked up to a Spring Valley police officer.

"When we got here, we saw a Negro male lying in the driveway. He didn't appear to be breathing. There was blood at his feet and on his clothing in the chest area. Annette was arrested. She told us she was protecting herself. My guess is she'll face a second-degree manslaughter charge."

September 1, 1981

Dan Walden said Indian Point was down again.

The plant spokesman said it was due to a pump that circulated the coolant water to the reactor.

"No, there's no danger to the public or to plant employees. The plant was shut at the time we discovered the malfunction. We're going to replace that pump motor. We're starting to do that and, um, we'll be down until at least the week of the twentieth of September."

For the first time, even Republican congressman Benjamin Gilman weighed in on Indian Point. "There's really no workable plan in place should there be a disaster. During the last congress, we worked with some of the representatives in the metropolitan area to press for an evacuation plan. I think the NRC should now be prepared to come forward with some decent planning, some protective measures so we can all be assured of some future safety. Over the years, I've been very much concerned that if we had something like Three Mile Island, people down to New York City could be greatly endangered."

September 2, 1981

I got pulled over by a Haverstraw cop for not making a full stop at a Stop sign. He looked at my driver's license.

"Are you the same Bob LeMoullec who works at WRKL?"

"Yes, that's me. I'm really sorry."

"All right, be more careful next time."

"Thank you."

I won't lie. I was very flattered when someone recognized my name. It happened all the time—now.

I sometimes got the false notion that I made it when I heard myself on the radio or when people you didn't know acted like you were special.

I was just amazed to be here.

Fifty-two

Sympathy for the Nazi

September 3, 1981

An immigration court finally got around to ordering a Nazi prison guard from New City deported.

Michael Gruber was eighty-four. He admitted he was a Waffen SS guard in Germany. He denied he served in the SS Death's Head Guard Battalion at the Sachenhausen concentration camp there.

A judge ruled Sachenhausen was one of the worst camps that brought death and human suffering to an untold number of Jews and gypsies.

The justice department said it had evidence Gruber was there in 1943 and 1944. I went to his house in New City to talk to him.

He lived very well in a posh neighborhood. America had been very good to him. Rich Lamb from WCBS got to the house the same time I did.

I had no use for Nazis. I had in the back of my mind what my future father-in-law went through at that time, watching his mother and two little sisters driven to their deaths. His father was killed not long afterward. My future father-in-law was fourteen when he was sent to Auschwitz where he stayed a short time before being transported from there to a slave labor camp.

Gruber looked old, even for eighty-four. He walked with two canes when he met us outside his front door.

I didn't know what to expect. He wouldn't deny the holocaust the way some freaks did. At the Nuremberg trials, the murderers who faced the death penalty or life behind bars didn't deny the holocaust. They said they were following orders. Maybe he'd tell me that. Maybe he'd be angry and yell at us to get off his property. That would be the best case.

I turned my tape recorder on. He waved me off. Then he spoke with a feeble voice. He was close to crying. "Please leave me alone. Can't you see I'm an old man? I'm very sick. Please let me be. Please."

How could I use the tape? He sounded so pathetic.

Many in our audience would hate me and be sympathetic to him.

Rich Lamb gave me a look. "I wouldn't use it."

He was right.

I did a couple of voicers and locked it out that I was in New City and left it at that.

September 4, 1981

There were a few of us in the newsroom when Bob Marvin appeared.

"I'm going to pitch a new account in Spring Valley. It's an upscale Mexican Restaurant called El Bandito."

I knew people who ate there. They loved it. At this point I'd have to be happy with Jack in the Box.

"Upscale, in Spring Valley?" Squiggy Panzarella chimed in.

"That's why I'm doing this one myself. This could be a big account. What's the honorary term for restaurant manager? I know in French it's maître d'."

"Try maricon."

A few hours later, Marvin came back flustered.

"I was met with a good deal of hostility. They have no chance of making it with that attitude."

September 6, 1981

A dead deer on Route 202 may have solved a related mystery. At one time, dozens of geese lived in the swamp behind the radio station. They became almost extinct.

A "concerned citizen" who left the post office that was next door to WRKL spotted two men putting Bambi's carcass into their car and driving it to a nearby Chinese restaurant.

The health department was called, and an inspector caught them red-handed butchering the animal. Now we're wondering if there's some connection to the missing geese.

Fifty-three

I Can Look Down and
Kiss the Sky

September 7, 1981

The hard work that set us apart from other radio stations paid off again. The Associated Press announced WRKL won five first place awards and two honorable mentions in this year's competition.

They also gave us the grand prize award for having the best radio news operation in New York State. We won this every year in recent memory.

Rich Mendelson said the judges were from Detroit so they had no iron in the fire. We did more than cover the sexy stories. There were school board, village board, town council, county legislature, zoning, and sewer district meetings too numerous to mention that we attended.

"They said WRKL's day-to-day coverage of its service area was nothing short of amazing, adding many newspapers could take a lesson from the way our radio station covers news."

We had a big staff that was complimented by some great freelancers, including Bill Cobb, Beth Robinson, Tobin Coleman, and Tony Winton.

September 9, 1981

My life was looking way up! I'd be married in a few days to one of the most beautiful women anywhere.

Here was the icing on the cake: the news director at WNEW AM and FM, Mike Prelee, sent me a response to my last inquiry, saying they're going to use my stories.

This was the home of William B. Williams, Scott Muni, Dave Herman, Bob Hagen, and other big leaguers.

Unless you were in the business, you probably couldn't understand the rejection virtually every one of us from top to bottom faced on a regular basis. We talked about it all the time among ourselves, but never with outsiders.

For every job you got, there were dozens of turndowns.

I could wallpaper my walls with rejection letters.

It turned out my wacky application worked. They'd take anything I could give them from Rockland and Westchester. My foot was in the door of the big time.

I knew it would happen! I was on my way!

Epilogue

Gary Axelbank has a cable TV show, "Bronx Talk." He's also director of public relations at Monroe College and is an associate athletic director.

Jeff Baker is an engineer at WNBC-TV.

Belton Brims was convicted of murder and escape in the Sohn Case. He's still serving his sentence for the New Jersey robberies at Rahway Prison. He won't start serving his seventy-five-year-to-life sentence in New York until 2018 at the earliest.

Bill Cobb was a trustee at SUNY Rockland when he passed away.

Tobin Coleman was Connecticut State Capitol correspondent for the Stamford Advocate and the Greenwich Times when he died while jogging in August 2006.

Bunny Crumpacker went on to write books on a wide range of subjects from jazz to cooking to a humorous history of numbers. She died in 2010 of cancer.

Dan Duprey is living the good life on eastern Long Island where he has been a news anchor at WLNG in Sag Harbor for more than twenty-five years.

Donna Donna is a DJ at WBAB on Long Island.

Sam Felder owns one of the biggest landscaping companies in Rockland County. He continued to call me for several years before he finally gave up.

Bruce Figler works at Creative Sound Works and DJs at 107.1, The Peak.

Eti and I visited Paul Giacobbe in the intensive care unit at Nyack Hospital shortly after he had a heart attack. He snuck out for a cigarette. Paul died six months later.

Ken Gribetz resigned after pleading guilty to federal misdemeanor charges of having employees drive him to private events and putting up a chupah on his property. He's currently a defense lawyer in Rockland County.

Jean Harris spent eleven years at the Bedford Correctional Facility where she educated female inmates. Her sentence was commuted by Governor Mario Cuomo. Harris died in 2012 of natural causes.

Rich Komonchak changed his on air name to Rich Thomason and is currently at Standard Radio News out of Washington, D.C.

Richard LaBarbara and Robert McCain are still serving life sentences in New York State prisons. Both continue to accuse the other of killing Paula Bohovesky.

Ray Lindemann lost his bid for reelection in November 1981.

Barrie Lipscomb left radio and, with her husband, took an active role in charitable causes too numerous to name here.

Bob Marvin was fired when WRKL became a union shop. He manages a shoe store in Paterson, New Jersey.

Neil Mazur is chief engineer at WAGA in Atlanta.

Rich Mendelson moved on to become the Associated Press's New York bureau chief.

Carl Nathe moved on to the University of Kentucky where he announces and does public relations.

Debbie Nigro has had a string of successful talk shows, the latest being the Debbie Nigro Show, which is on the web and on WFAS-AM and WGCH.

Paul "Squiggy" Panzerella is a karate instructor in Texas.

Dave Peters went to the Associated Press.

Steve Possell has a morning talk show at WRCR in Rockland County.

Ron Rizzi is no longer in broadcasting.

Steve Roy got sober and went on to become the number-one-rated afternoon DJ in the country at Lite-FM in NYC. He's currently a successful financial planner at Prudential.

Beth Robinson became vice president of CBS news before heading the communications department at SUNY Rockland.

Sandy Rubenstein's law firm takes on high-profile civil rights cases, most notably Abner Louima's.

Barry Sachs is now a senior coordinating producer at ESPN.

Tim Scheld became a correspondent for ABC News Radio. He's currently news director at WCBS-AM in New York City.

James Sheffield was arrested in California in 1982. He was convicted of the Sohn murders and is still incarcerated in New York.

Lori Siegel left the business to go to Touro Law School on Long Island. The last I heard, she was an executive producer at Court TV and TruTV where she supervised and developed over five hundred programs including Forensic Files and Investigators.

Ralph Snodsmith moved his Garden Hotline show to WOR in New York City. He died in 2010.

Sheryl Sohn spent twenty-six years in prison where she turned her life around. She's currently counseling women at a halfway house in Brooklyn.

Vin the cat met his maker when he tried to cross Route 202 in front of the radio station. He was buried in the back parking lot.

Ken Voight worked as a reporter at 1010 WINS and a reporter/producer at WNBC before retiring.

Evan Weiner has authored several books and makes the rounds talking about the business of sports on a number of network talk shows.

Linda Winikow lost her chance in Albany when she supported Ed Koch over Mario Cuomo in a gubernatorial race. She took an executive post at Orange and Rockland Utilities. It was there she tried to become a king maker, doling out campaign contributions to candidates she believed were worthy. Prosecutors said she crossed the line. She pled guilty to influence peddling and other charges in 1993 and served six months in the Rockland County Jail. Linda died in 2008. She was sixty-eight.

Tony Winton is a reporter and heads the Associated Press's Miami bureau. He's also president of the News Media Guild.

Amer Zada is still serving a life term at a New York state prison.

Samir Zada was released in 2014 and was deported to

Jordan. Their brother Nazir died when a balloon filled with heroin he tried to smuggle to one of his brothers burst in his stomach.

Dave Zechnowitz, who wouldn't go on tape when he called in the Sohn murder, had a talk show under the name Freddie Mertz at the ABC Radio Network. He still occasionally does talk shows while teaching high school in New Jersey and working as a reporter at Gannett newspapers.

Doctor Frederick Zugibe who modernized forensic pathology in Rockland County went on to pen a number of books. He won international acclaim for his work on the burial cloth of Jesus and his scientific research on Jesus's death. He died in 2013 at age eighty-five.

His son, Thomas Zugibe, who was put on a cross as part of Dr. Zugibe's research, is currently the Rockland County district attorney.

WRNW is now called 107.1 the peak after several incarnations. It's an extremely well-programmed local radio station.

WRKL was sold to a Polish-American broadcasting company which simulcasts Polish programming by satellite from Chicago.

A number of household names in New York City and in some instances around the country worked at WRKL after I left. They include Sean Adams, George Bodarky, Mary Calvi, Chris Carlin, Joe Clines, Kevin Connors, Melissa Conti, Tanya Hansen, Pam Puso, Scott Salotto, Adam Schein, Andrew Schmertz, Scott Stanford, Steve Wendell, and John Wilson.

Eti and I continued to live in Rockland County where we had five children and seven grandchildren. I eventually made it to 1010 WINS where I worked as a writer, reporter, and editor for about seventeen years before moving on to television at Fox News.

In the interim, I became news director at WRKL and at WFAS AM and FM. I was a freelance reporter and writer at the ABC Radio networks, CNN, the Associated Press, United Press International, and the *New York Post*. I was greatly helped along the way by top flight news people I worked for including Mike Eisgrau at WNEW, Kathleen Maloney (another WRKL alum) and Tom Romano at WABC AM, Doug O'Brien and Bill Maher (father of the HBO host) at WNBC AM, and Mike Bennett at WHUD.

I retired and currently teach broadcast writing at Rockland Community College.

About the Author

Bob LeMoullec currently teaches Broadcast Writing to college students at SUNY Rockland.

He began his radio journey full time at WRKL-AM where he became News Director. He worked on the air at a number of stations including WRNW-FM, WFAS-AM and FM, WLNA-AM, and WHUD-FM. He did freelance reporting at the Associated Press, UPI, ABC Radio Networks, WNBC-AM, WABC-AM, and the New York Post before moving on to all-news 1010 WINS in New York City.

Bob then joined Fox News as a television news producer.

He has won outright or shared in more than thirty news awards from the AP, UPI, New York State Broadcasters Association and the Radio and Television News Directors Association.

Bob also contributed to "Covering Catastrophe," which recounted the story of September 11 in the words of the broadcast journalists who covered it.

He has five children, seven grandchildren, and lives with his wife of thirty-two years in a suburb of New York City.

To book clubs and groups with 10 or more members:

I will address, in person, any gathering in the New York metropolitan area. Write to newsman13@aol.com for information.

CPSIA information can be obtained at www.ICGtesting.com
Printed in the USA
LVOW07s1609110115

422375LV00007B/708/P

9 781628 386325